HOT Topics

YOUTH ELECTIVES

School
Male & Female
Doubts

David C. Cook Publishing Co.
Elgin, Illinois / Weston, Ontario

Hot Topics Youth Electives: School, Male and Female, and Doubts

© 1989 David C. Cook Publishing Co.

Scripture quotations are from the *Holy Bible: New International Version* (NIV), © 1973, 1978, 1984 by the New York International Bible Society. Used by permission of Zondervan Bible Publishers.

Published by David C. Cook Publishing Co.
850 N. Grove Ave., Elgin, IL 60120
Cable address: DCCOOK
Designed by Randy Maid
Illustrated by John Duckworth and Randy Maid
Photo by Bill Bilsley
Printed in U.S.A.

ISBN: 1-55513-202-2

CONTENTS

What's So Hot about Hot Topics?

Let's face it: You want the kids in your youth group or Sunday School class to *like* you. Sure, you want to be respected, but you want to be liked, too—at least a little.

That's why you cringe when you're called upon to teach or lead a session on a topic you know your kids will hate—say, Sibbecai the Hushathite in I Chronicles. You know you'll have to dress up that topic with funny hats, run relay races around it, and serve banana splits afterward just to keep kids from using that dreaded word—*boring*—about you.

It doesn't seem fair, does it? You do all that work, and kids turn up their noses just because they can't instantly relate to the topic.

You deserve a break. That's why we created Hot Topics Youth Electives.

Hot Sessions

First, we picked the subjects most kids are already thinking about—things like TV and movies, sports, music, feelings, school, and sexuality. That's so you can announce, "Hey, kids—next week we're going to talk about TV and movies!" Sounds better than Sibbecai the Hushathite any day, doesn't it?

Then we got some of the country's most experienced writers of youth programming to come up with sessions that explore those hot topics. We gave those writers a challenge: to create sessions that were full of creative activities *and* substantial Bible content. Each session would have to be usable in Sunday School *and* youth group, aimed at high schoolers but adaptable to junior high. Preparation would have to be easy, too—no forcing the leader to collect 300 bottle caps, two films, and an armadillo to do the session.

It was a tall order, but they did it.

Hot Tips

Next we contacted some of the most respected youth workers and speakers around—people like Tony Campolo, Duffy Robbins, Tim Stafford, and Barbara Varenhorst. We asked them to tell you how to approach these hot topics with your kids. We told them to think of themselves as friendly advisors sitting across the kitchen table from you. The resulting how-to articles would help you get ready for each unit of sessions.

That was a tall order, too—but they came through with flying colors.

Hot Format

There was still one thing left to do. We had to make sure each book was easy to follow. So we clearly marked each session's aim, key verses, and materials at the start (we called them The Point, The Passages, and the Preparation). We gave every step in the session a title and goal of its own. We put instructions to you in regular type, things you might say to kids in bold type, and suggested answers in parentheses.

We also put reproducible student sheets at the end of each unit of sessions. That's so you don't have to buy separate student books or worksheets.

Have It Your Way!

These sessions aren't just hot. They're flexible. They're active enough for youth group meetings and retreats, biblical enough for Sunday School. You can use this book in all sorts of ways. For instance:

• Use it for a 13-week quarter, leading the 12 regular sessions and one of the bonus sessions.

• Use it for a month at a time, working your way through a topic for four or five weeks.

• Use single sessions whenever you need them.

In other words, you can use them any time you want to get kids talking about—and applying biblical principles to—their favorite subjects.

Do that, and you may become one of their favorite leaders. And next time you have to talk about Sibbecai the Hushathite, they may even listen.

Have a hot time with these topics!

—*John Duckworth, Editor*

How to Talk to Kids About School

by Guy Doud

How can you discuss the trials and triumphs of school life with the kids in your class or group? Should you mention the "good old days" of your own adolescence and wear your musty letter sweater? Or should you be so hip that the principal would mistake you for a current sophomore?

Talking to kids about school isn't a matter of finding exactly the right outfit, style, or even words. It's not a specialized art or science, and it doesn't require re-enrolling in classes yourself. In fact, it involves the same basic skills used in talking to kids about *anything*. Discussing grades, stress, time management, making the most of school, witnessing, and other issues facing kids today simply requires knowing how to communicate effectively.

Here are five basic principles that help me—and will help you—get through to young people.

Be Informed

Not long ago I heard a speaker go on and on about the evils of contemporary rock music. "Our kids are being corrupted," he said, "by groups like the Beatles, and by people like Alice Cooper."

The Beatles and Alice Cooper?

It was apparent that the speaker knew little about current trends in popular music—or about kids today.

That's a problem many adults have in communicating with kids about school. Often we're not adequately informed about the world of the adolescent—and sometimes we don't want to be informed. We don't want to believe that the kids from our church could be doing what "other kids" are doing.

That's unfortunate, because the first rule of effective communication is to know your audience. Your students are unique, with special school-related needs. They also have their own levels of spiritual maturity, and it helps to be realistic about that. It sure would be nice if they all knew the Ten Commandments by heart and spent hours every day reading the Word, but that's probably not the case!

To get through to kids, try to meet them where they are and take it from there. Jesus had a wonderful way of doing this. Remember how He told the truth to the woman at the well (John 4)? He knew her situation, didn't avoid the specifics, and was able to communicate with her.

Find out as much as you can about your kids and what they face at school. It isn't hard. Just look—and open your ears. It's amazing how much kids will tell you if you just ask—and listen without comment. Let them know you really care about what's going on at school. They'll respond.

You'll probably find it helpful to visit a local school—as well as other places where kids hang out and commiserate about their teachers and tests. Keeping up with the general youth culture is a good idea, too; try reading some youth magazines, including reviews of the latest records, tapes, and compact discs. If kids see that you understand their culture, vocabulary, and trends, they'll be far more receptive to you than they would be to an adult they think is "out of it."

One student told me about a friend of his who had made a "bong"—a pipe for smoking drugs—in pottery class at school. The art teacher didn't know what a bong was. The student told this story to the school counselor, who didn't know what it was, either. The student's derisive comment to me: "He didn't even know what a bong was, man!"

You don't need to compromise your standards to be informed. But it's essential to know your audience.

Be Yourself

Being informed doesn't mean trying to act "cool," however. Too many people who work with kids try to impress them. You can't fool kids; they can spot a phony, and they know you're not in high school anymore. You don't have to dress the way they dress, talk the way they talk, or even like their music. Let them know what you're really like. They'll respect you for that.

Try telling kids what it was like for you when you went to school. Talk about how things are different now. Ask kids what they think school will be like for *their* children; that makes them think a little!

If you're sincere, if you let kids know you care about them, if you admit you don't understand everything, if you ask questions because you really want to know—then kids will tell you more than you ever expected. Kids know that you are not a kid, and that is okay with them. They appreciate it when you are honest about who you are and what you believe.

Be a Challenger

The church needs to be a place where kids are challenged to be disciples of our Lord Jesus Christ. They need to be taught what a disciple is, and what it means to be one at school.

Some leaders skip such challenges and try only to entertain their young people. I recently spoke to a church youth group whose "youth ministry" activity for the week was to rent the movie *Dirty Dancing* on video! You don't need to compete with the media—or with school for that matter. Kids need to be confronted with the truth of the Gospel. They need to know that your emphasis is not on entertaining them, but rather on helping them learn that Jesus wants them to lead the lives of servants—at school and elsewhere.

That's definitely a challenge in an age when many people think the goal of school is preparing students to go into the world and make as much money as they can. Christian kids need to be reminded of Christ's plea to remember "the least of these My brethren." When you talk with kids about school, try encouraging them to see how their studies and skills might be used to further the cause of Christ.

Be an Example

The best "talk" is silent. If we really want to talk to kids about school, we need to demonstrate to them a consistent lifestyle that shows how to live as a Christian in the weekday world. In the words of a poem that's greatly influenced my thinking about communicating with kids, "I'd rather *see* a sermon than *hear* one any day."

As the apostle Paul wrote, "You yourselves are our letter, written on our hearts, known and read by everybody. You show that you are a letter from Christ, the result of our ministry, written not with ink but with the Spirit of the living God, not on tablets of stone but on tablets of human hearts" (II Corinthians 3:2, 3). When we realize that our examples are being written on the tablets of teenagers' hearts, and that those teenagers are going into school every week where they can influence others, the responsibility is rather over-whelming.

We who work with young people must present ourselves as examples—not as perfected saints, but as women and men who have fought the fight against the things of the world and have opted

for the things of God. When we do this we have our best chance of helping kids to be effective witnesses for Christ at school.

Be Patient

Finally, if we want to talk effectively with kids about school, we must be patient. Kids are kids. God is not finished with anybody yet—especially young people. They *and* we need to realize that.

No matter what kids have thought or done or failed to do at school, Christ is bigger than their failures. He wants to take away sin, and not just for a short spell. He'll remove it forever! In the same way that God is patient with His children, we must be patient with our students.

As you talk with your precious young people about school, remember that any one of them could represent our Lord (Matthew 25:35-40). If you follow that advice alone, you'll have no trouble communicating with them about school—or anything else.

Guy Doud, a popular speaker to youth and youth workers, was named National High School Teacher of the Year for 1986-87. He is also pastor of Christ Community Church, Nisswa, Minnesota.

by Ben Sharpton

Ben Sharpton is a freelance writer and youth worker in Central Florida. He's published over 100 articles in a variety of Christian and secular publications, and for over 15 years he's been actively involved in youth ministry.

"There is a growing awareness and growing incidence of psychological stress on children," says Dr. David Elkind, author of *The Hurried Child*. "Exposing kids to more at younger ages is clearly not working. It doesn't 'build character'—it creates stress."

If we think adults are the only ones who face stress daily, our memories are faulty. Remember the pressure to get homework done? How about the "drowning" sensation of not being able to understand geometry or sentence diagramming? If you attended a large school, you may have felt the stress of being a forgotten cog in a giant, gray machine. Then there were the stresses of trying to be liked, trying to make the team, trying to keep your grades up so you could "get a good job someday."

Most schools—and the people in them—press kids to perform and conform. In junior high and high school the pressure often gets worse. This session is designed to help kids name their own school-related stresses and start matching those stresses with biblical coping principles.

Surviving the System

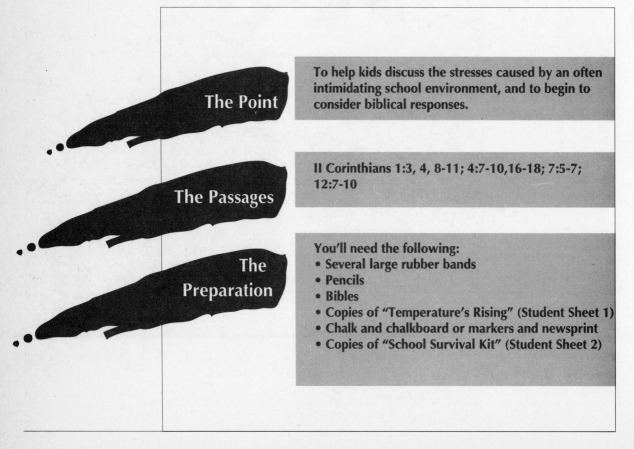

The Point

To help kids discuss the stresses caused by an often intimidating school environment, and to begin to consider biblical responses.

The Passages

II Corinthians 1:3, 4, 8-11; 4:7-10,16-18; 7:5-7; 12:7-10

The Preparation

You'll need the following:
• Several large rubber bands
• Pencils
• Bibles
• Copies of "Temperature's Rising" (Student Sheet 1)
• Chalk and chalkboard or markers and newsprint
• Copies of "School Survival Kit" (Student Sheet 2)

The Pressure Cooker
Identifying School Stress

As students arrive, pass out copies of "Temperature's Rising" (Student Sheet 1). Ask kids to examine the items at the top of the page and consider how much pressure these cause in their lives. Each student should write these items on the thermometer at the point that best shows how much "heat" or pressure it exerts on him or her (100 degrees centigrade represents the "boiling point" and 0 degrees represents "freezing").

For example, if competition for grades causes a lot of stress, a student might write that at the 95-degree mark. A kid who isn't involved in sports may choose to write "sports" at the 10-degree mark. Give everyone time to write down all the items. While kids are completing the exercise, write the items on chalkboard or newsprint.

Ask each person to call out his or her temperature ratings one at a time. Write these on the blackboard or newsprint beside the corresponding stress categories. Total the numbers beside each category, divide by the number of students in your group, and write down that number—the average degree of stress caused by that item for the whole group—to the left of the categories. Have students compare their stress levels with the group averages.

Which items cause the most stress for people in this group?

Which cause the least?

Would you say the averages apply to most kids in your school? Why or why not?

Stretch, But Don't Snap
Telling the Difference between Good and Bad Tension

Ask two volunteers to conduct a simple demonstration at the front of the room. Give them a handful of pencils and a large rubber band; the rubber band should be too long to hold the pencils together in a bundle without having to be doubled over.

Challenge your volunteers to bind the pencils in a bundle with the rubber band—without stretching the rubber band in any way. They won't be able to do it, since doubling the band would require stretching it.

Now tell them they can stretch the rubber band in order to bundle the pencils. It shouldn't take them long to do it. Say something like, **Sometimes you have to stretch to get the job done. Within reason, tension can be a good thing. We had to create tension in this rubber band to get it to hold the pencils together. Without any tension at all, things can fall apart.**

Give the volunteers another rubber band. Have them grasp the ends of it and move apart, stretching it to its limits and beyond. After it breaks, say, **If there's too much tension, things break. If we tried to use that rubber band to bundle the pencils now, it wouldn't work too well. Too much stress can cause permanent damage.**

Thank the volunteers. Use the following questions to help your group consider the positive and negative sides of tension (in students, not rubber bands):

When can tension at school be good? (Some possibilities: When it keeps you alert, helps you do your best, makes you think about a tough issue, or reminds you to rely on God.)

When can tension be destructive? (When it makes you so nervous you can't function; when it makes you sick; when it keeps you from enjoying school, making friends, or learning.)

How can you tell when tension is hurting you? (Some people get skin ailments, digestive problems, headaches, or backaches; you may be afraid to go to school or want to drop out; you might snap at family or friends; your grades might fall; you might feel tired or nervous much of the time.)

Ask kids whether they think the following situations represent good tension or bad tension and why. Some of them are tough to call, so "right" answers aren't required. Discuss whether your kids have faced these or other stressful situations.

1. Your stomach is in knots because you didn't study for today's test.

2. You hate going to P.E. class because you're embarrassed to take a shower with the other kids.

3. You feel nervous as you prepare to try out for a school play, team, or band.

4. You want to drop out of school because most of the classes seem "over your head."

5. You're afraid to walk down a certain hall at school because of the kids who gather there.

Pressure Points
Examining Causes of School Stress

Circle the three items that received the highest average scores in Step 1. These are the three largest producers of school pressures for your group. Divide the group into three teams of about equal size. Assign one of the three high-pressure areas to each group.

Each group should work together to decide how the following can ease our school stress in that area or make it worse:
- Ourselves
- School system
- Teachers
- Friends
- Other kids who aren't friends
- Parents
- People at church
- God

Have groups report their findings to the rest of the class. If they have trouble being specific about how God can help, observe that you'll be looking into that during the rest of the session.

Paul under Pressure
Discovering Paul's Stresses and Responses

Draw attention again to the three highest stressors identified earlier in this session. Explain that these are often the result of a competitive and impersonal school system.

The apostle Paul often struggled with stressful, impersonal systems like the Roman government and Jewish and Christian groups that were tied down by tradition. He faced plenty of physical stress, too—including shipwreck, poisonous snakes, attempted murder, and being thrown in prison. In the midst of one of these struggles he wrote to the church at Corinth. Here are

some of the things he had to say.

Assign the three teams from Step 3 to read and discuss the following passages, all of which are from II Corinthians. What does each passage have to say about Paul's reaction to stress? What seemed to keep Paul going? What was there about being a Christian that helped him through trouble? Then regather the group and share observations. As needed, add the comments that follow the verses.

Team A

1:3, 4: God cares about our stressful situations and comforts us; He brings good out of trouble by enabling us to comfort others who go through the same things.

1:8-11: Paul faced extreme, even deadly, stress. But through it he learned to rely on God, not on himself. Looking back on that experience gave him confidence that God would see him through in the future, too. The prayers of other people also helped Paul endure stress.

Team B

4:7-10: When Paul counted on God in stressful times, he was showing others that power comes from God, not from us. When we're trusting Christ, stress may put us down, but not out. It can press but not crush us, confuse us but not force us to give up, strike us down but not destroy us. God will never abandon us. Belonging to Christ can make us walking examples of the way He brings life out of death—or new strength out of stress.

4:16-18: If we keep our eyes on what lasts forever—our relationship with God, for instance—it gives us perspective on the stress that seems so terrible now. Stress wears us down every day, but God can keep refreshing us just as often.

Team C

7:5-7: Sources of stress include lack of rest, harassment and conflict with others, and our own fears. God can comfort us in these situations through the presence of people who care about us.

12:7-10: Paul faced the continuing stress of a physical problem that wouldn't go away no matter how much he prayed about it. Paul saw that as a chance to show God's power at work. He was "weak" so that God's strength could be demonstrated.

What practical ideas for dealing with stress can we get from Paul's experience? (Some possibilities: Use your stressful experience to help somebody else who has a similar problem; rely on God rather than trying to deal with it all by yourself; find someone who'll pray for you; remember how God has helped you through stress before; remember that God won't abandon you; keep your eyes on what lasts forever and remember that most stresses are temporary; give God a chance to renew you daily by spending time with Him; get enough rest and do what you can to live peacefully with others; let others who care about you help you; instead of giving up if God doesn't take the stress away, ask Him to show His strength by helping you through it.)

School Survival Kit

Identifying Resources to Help Us Survive School Stress

Pass out copies of "School Survival Kit" (Student Sheet 2). Have individuals complete the sheets, naming at least four of their personal resources if possible. Fill out a sheet yourself, based on things that helped or could have helped you as a teenager at school. Offer the following examples, as well as your own, to encourage the sharing of what kids have written:

• An older sister might give you advice on how to study for a particular class or get along with a certain teacher.

• A prayer partner could help you feel less alone in a big school or pray for specific needs.

• A song like "El Shaddai" running through your head could keep reminding you of God's power and protection as you face a hostile classmate.

Encourage kids to take their "How he or she might help" answers to the people they named, asking for their support in coping with school stress. You might want to volunteer to be a prayer partner or friend.

If possible, close by having kids pray for each other's stress-related concerns.

The SAT (Scholastic Aptitude Test) scores of American students began to drop in 1967. In 1980 scores leveled off and have been rising gradually since then. But at this writing they haven't reached the high established in 1967.

Experts say the response to this decline will affect the future of the U.S. economy and government. That puts pressure on schools, who put pressure on kids. Many parents also drive kids to get good grades, knowing that low grades jeopardize college admission, scholarships, and job opportunities. The U.S. isn't alone; competition is even tougher in countries like Japan and Korea.

How do teenagers respond? Some seem to take the pressure without damage. But others burn out, drop out, rebel, or establish patterns of cheating that can last the rest of their lives.

This session will help you discuss in a biblical light the topics of grades, teachers, cheating, and competition. Be sure it's a discussion, though; encourage all who want to participate. Rare is the student who has no opinion on these subjects—and no problems with them.

This Is a Test

The Point

To help kids discuss their views of teachers and grades, and to help them discover biblical alternatives to rebellion, cheating, and over-competition.

The Passages

Luke 2:39-52; Romans 13:1-5; Proverbs 21:2, 3, 6, 8; Matthew 6:25-34

The Preparation

You'll need the following:
• Copies of "Teacher Report Card" (Student Sheet 3)
• Pencils
• Bibles
• Blackboard and chalk or newsprint and markers
• Copies of "Cheating Test" (Student Sheet 4)

Step 1

Teacher Report Card
Evaluating Those Who Teach Us

Pass out copies of "Teacher Report Card" (Student Sheet 3) to kids as they arrive. Tell them it's time to grade their teachers. At the top of the report card is a spot for them to place a letter grade they would give their teachers this year. Give them time to write in that grade. If kids find it hard to give an overall grade because they like some teachers and can't stand others, have them give individual grades, average them, and write the result on the sheet.

Beneath the letter grade are several characteristics of teachers. Ask students to place a check mark in the first column beside each characteristic they feel is important in a good teacher. If their teachers have generally displayed that trait, students should mark the second column, too.

Collect the report cards and have a volunteer tally the letter grade results—how many kids put A's, B's, C's, etc. in the spot at the top. While he or she does that, share the following findings from a 1987 survey of high school seniors by *Phi Delta Kappan* Magazine (March, 1987):

In this national study, 8.2% of the seniors gave their teachers a grade of "A" and 44.3% granted them a "B" grade. Only 1% of these students said they would fail their teachers.

Ask your volunteer to share the tally results. Compare these with the national averages. Let kids suggest reasons for differences.

Next, ask your volunteer to determine which characteristics of teachers were checked most often in column one on the report cards. Have a second student determine which traits were checked most often in column two. While your statisticians are tallying, share these national findings and write them on chalkboard or newsprint:

The top three characteristics identified by seniors in the 1987 survey were understanding (82%), knowledge (81%), and fairness (79%). But the top three characteristics that were *demonstrated* by teachers, according to the same students, were knowledge (87%), friendliness (80%), and competence (75%). Understanding—the number one characteristic as chosen by 82% of the respondents—was demonstrated only 66% of the time.

Ask your volunteers to report the top characteristics in both columns as determined by the group. Compare these to the national statistics.

Which traits would you like to see more often in your teachers?
Which would you like to see less often?
What traits would you add to the list on the report card? Why?

Step 2

The Trouble with Grades
Examining Our Examination Methods

Ask these questions to help your group think about the grading system at school:

Do the grades you just gave your teachers really show how competent they are?

Do your own grades at school really show how well you've mastered a subject?

After a few responses, explain that you're going to make several statements about grades. Kids should agree or disagree by giving a "thumbs up" or "thumbs down" sign after each statement. Pause after each vote to allow kids to explain their reasons. The resulting discussion may help you identify some of their grade-related struggles.

Statements:

1. Grades put too much pressure on most students.

2. My teachers grade too strictly.

3. Grading on a curve is a bad idea.

4. Students who get a "D" on a subject shouldn't be allowed to play school sports.

5. Students should never be held back a year because they flunked.

6. My parents worry more about grades than I do.

7. Grades promote cheating.

8. You can get good grades without learning.

9. There should be a national grading system for high school students.

10. You can get a good job even if you don't get good grades.

Wrap up this discussion by asking each student to make a one-sentence opinion statement about teachers or grades. If some kids would rather not make a statement, avoid pressuring them.

Teachers, Principals, and Principles
Discovering Biblical Ways to See School Authorities

Split the group into two teams, "junior varsity" and "varsity," according to age. Have each team study a Scripture passage as follows.

Junior Varsity:

This team reads Luke 2:39-52, which tells how Jesus, as a boy, amazed the teachers in Jerusalem. The team should, based on this passage, come up with three statements Jesus might have made about teachers and learning.

Varsity:

This team reads Romans 13:1-5, in which Paul describes the Christian's relationship to government. The team should create three statements Paul might have made about teachers and other school authorities.

When teams are done, bring the whole group back together. Ask team spokespersons to write responses on the chalkboard or newsprint. Team members should explain how they came up with their statements. As needed, supplement the discussion with the following.

Junior Varsity:

1. Gaining wisdom (having sound judgment), not just knowledge (knowing facts), is important (vss. 40, 52).

2. We should listen to teachers and ask them questions (vs. 46).

3. Talk with teachers and respectfully offer opinions (vs. 46).

4. We need to understand what we learn, not just know the right answers (vs. 47).

5. We shouldn't act as if we know it all, even if we're at the top of the class (vss. 46, 47).

6. Knowing a lot doesn't mean we don't have to obey and respect those over us (vs. 51).

You might point out that Jesus didn't seem to view teachers as figures to be hated or feared, in contrast to the way some kids feel today. And there's nothing in the passage to indicate that these teachers were perfect—or even especially knowledgeable or understanding.

Varsity:

1. Every student is to obey school rules (vs. 1).

2. Submit to teachers and principals (vss. 1, 2).

3. God places school authorities in their positions (vs. 1).

4. We obey school authorities because we want to obey God, not just to avoid punishment (vss. 1, 2, 5).

5. Generally, if you do the right thing you won't get in trouble (vss. 3, 4).

6. God allows school authorities to punish wrongdoers (vs. 4).

Observe that a school rule or authority might tell us to do something wrong—though that doesn't happen too often in our society. When it does, "We must obey God rather than men" (Acts 5:29).

Compare the teams' statements with the ones kids made earlier about teachers and learning. Which agree? Which are different?

Let's say you have a teacher who's unfair. What do you think Jesus and Paul would want you to do?

After giving kids a chance to respond, observe that Jesus did criticize some teachers of the Law when He was an adult. But He was a teacher, too, as well as being the Son of God. He asked God to forgive even those who were putting Him to death, so He would probably say to forgive the teacher and try to make peace with him or her. Paul told Christians to submit to the Roman government, one of the most oppressive in history, so he would probably say to submit to unfair teachers, too. That means having a loving attitude, too, not griping when the teacher's out of earshot.

Cheaters Never Prosper?
Discussing the Temptation to Cheat for Grades

Announce that you're going to have a test. Distribute copies of "Cheating Test" (Student Sheet 4) and have kids write in answers as directed on the sheet. Discuss the results. Most of the answers will reflect opinions, but the last question should draw principles like these from the Proverbs verses:

• We might excuse cheating, but God knows the truth (vs. 2).

• Doing what's right and just (fair) is God's top priority for us; cheating is wrong because it involves lying about your work, and it's unfair to those who *earn* their grades (vs. 3).

• We may think we have to cheat to get into college and a high-paying job, but the effects of cheating last longer than the rewards (vs. 6).

• Cheating makes us guilty of being devious, and God wants us to be innocent and upright (vs. 8).

Safety Valve
Remembering That God Is Bigger Than Grades

Ask students to close their eyes and think about their last report cards—or final exams, if these are approaching. As kids keep their eyes closed, say something along these lines:

Trying to get good grades makes some people worry a lot. Maybe their parents pressure them. Maybe they pressure themselves. Some kids feel they have to cheat just to keep up.

Getting good grades is worthwhile, but worrying and cheating aren't. Studying and getting help from teachers can bring your grades up, but worrying can't. Listen to what Jesus had to say about worry, and think about what it might have to do with grades.

Read Matthew 6:25-34 aloud. Then close in prayer.

Are teenagers busy? Check out these U.S. statistics from a recent survey:

Over 10 million people age 7 through 17 said they played organized basketball.

Nearly 8 million played baseball.

Over 6 million young people played soccer, and the same number enjoyed volleyball.

Organized football was played by 6.2 million children and teens.

Then there are the youth organizations:

YMCA serves almost 7 million kids.

The Boy Scouts of America have 3.5 million young people involved.

The Girl Scouts of America boast 200,000 participants.

Over 500,000 high school students are involved in 4-H.

And what about band, drama, speech teams, and after-school jobs—not to mention church activities? No wonder so many kids have trouble getting "little things" like schoolwork done.

Not all teenagers are swamped with extracurricular activities, of course. And in many rural and urban areas, there aren't *enough* organized activities to keep kids off the streets. But for those who need help deciding the best ways to use their time, this session provides practice as well as principles.

The 25-Hour Day

The Point

To help kids prioritize their use of time with biblical values in mind.

The Passages

Exodus 18:13-27; Ephesians 5:15-17; Luke 10:38-42

The Preparation

You'll need the following:
- Paper, pencils
- Bibles
- A couple of old high school yearbooks, preferably yours
- Copies of "Letter to Larry" (Student Sheet 5)
- Copies of "Time Management Tips" (Student Sheet 6)
- Chalkboard and chalk or newsprint and markers

Times Have Changed
Listing the Activities We Have to Choose From

Bring a couple of old high school yearbooks—preferably your own—to the session. Give kids a chance to examine them as the session begins. Expect remarks about fashions, fads, etc.

After a few minutes, create with kids a list of "extinct" extracurricular activities that were offered in your day but aren't today. Jot these on chalkboard or newsprint. Then list activities that weren't offered when you were in school, but are today. Jot these in another column.

Were there more extracurricular activities in the "old" days, or fewer?
Do you think it's tougher to get your homework done today, or easier?
Is it harder or easier to decide how to use your time today?

Listen to kids' opinions. Offer your own if you wish. Then collect the yearbooks so that students aren't distracted by them during the rest of the session.

What Are You Doing?
Identifying Things That Take up Our Time

Pass out paper and pencils. Have each student make a "What Am I Doing?" list of time-consuming activities. Start with the broad categories of school and homework. Each person should also write down all the extracurricular activities he or she is involved in—church activities, entertainment, jobs, sports, clubs, etc.

After kids finish their lists, have them write down the number of hours they typically spend on each activity in a week. Students may have to guess on some of the activities, but challenge them to be as accurate as possible.

Then ask the following questions to help group members come to grips with their use of time:

How do you decide how to spend your time?
Do you feel that you control your time—or does your time control you?
Is there some activity (besides school) that receives an unnecessarily large chunk of your time?
Which activities on your list could you do without? Which require more time than you are now able to give?

Clockwise
Discussing God's View of Spending Time

Ask someone to read aloud Ephesians 5:15-17. Discuss two of the main points of the passage—making the most of every opportunity and understanding the Lord's will—along the following lines.

What's the difference between making the most of every opportunity and signing up for every activity you hear about? (Signing up for everything makes you busy, but it doesn't guarantee that you'll enjoy yourself or do a good job. Sometimes you can't make the most of one project if you're distracted by two or three others.)

Most people think of opportunities as chances to get more money,

power, or fame. **How is that different from the opportunities in this passage?** (These are opportunities to do the Lord's will [vs. 17].)

How can you tell what the Lord's will is when it comes to deciding to take on projects? (Some ideas: Think about how it will affect family, friends, and other commitments; study the Bible regularly so you understand its counsel before a question comes up; stay close to God so that His will is important to you; talk to mature Christians you know; pray about it.)

Here are some opportunities. Which ones do you think could be turned into chances to glorify God? Why?

1. Writing an editorial for the school newspaper.

2. *Failing* to make the basketball team.

3. Trying out for a play.

4. Running for vice-president of the student body.

5. Spending your junior year in Europe.

6. Attending a youth Bible study.

7. Working after school in a fast-food place where most of the other employees aren't Christians.

(All could be opportunities to glorify God—if we decide to use them that way. The point is that the Lord's will for our activities involves our motives, not just the activities themselves.)

Now let's say you're faced with all these opportunities at the same time. How do you decide which ones to do first, which ones to put off, and which ones to forget? (You have to decide which are most important; that means setting priorities.)

Moses had a problem like this. Let's see what he did.

Desert Dilemma

Discovering How Moses Set His Priorities

During the Exodus from Egypt, Moses faced a real time crunch. He was so busy settling other people's arguments that he was wearing himself out. His father-in-law gave him some excellent advice (as fathers-in-law like to do). Listen to this story and try to determine what the most important parts of that advice were.

Have someone read aloud Exodus 18:13-27.

After the passage is read, have the group glean principles of time management from the story. List these on the chalkboard or newsprint.

Some possibilities:

1. Remember that God is with you.

2. Realize that it's not good to wear yourself out.

3. Divide your tasks into chunks that are easier to handle.

4. Delegate responsibilities; don't try to do everything yourself.

5. Set priorities; work on the important tasks and stop doing the unimportant ones.

6. Follow through; don't just listen to advice and not do anything about it.

Moses learned that some things were better left to other people. What are some extracurricular activities that are especially tough to leave to others? (Things that will make us look good; fun activities; projects we fear others will mess up; jobs that would make us money, etc.)

Dear Larry

Practice Setting Priorities

Just List

Pass out copies of "Letter to Larry" (Student Sheet 5). Tell kids to read the case study carefully and to write a brief letter giving Larry advice on how to manage his time, drawing on ideas discussed so far in this session. Letters should include a list of suggested priorities for Larry, from the most important to the least.

Have volunteers read their letters aloud. Compare the priorities and ask students to explain how they reached their conclusions.

The School Board Meeting (optional):

Simulating a Conflict of Priorities

If time allows, announce that you're going to have a very brief, simulated school board meeting. During this meeting, each student is assigned the role of a school board member. Begin by assigning the role of chairperson.

The board has three important issues to settle during this meeting:

1. Students have requested that six school clubs, similar to college fraternities, be established. Each club would have a variety of parties and service projects. Membership would be selected by students who start the clubs.

2. A motion has been made to suspend athletes from sports teams if their grade averages fall below "C." If the motion is passed, seven players on one local high school football team would not be able to play.

3. A non-denominational Christian organization has requested permission to bring adult workers on campus during school hours—and to have Bible Studies with interested students every morning one hour before school starts.

Let your "school board" work to resolve these issues. Choose just one or two issues if time is short. Help kids see how their values (fairness, need for education, participation in sports, tolerance, spreading the Gospel, etc.) determine their priorities—which determine how they spend their time.

First Things Last

Remembering Our Most Important Activity

Read Luke 10:38-42. Note that Jesus cared that Martha was harassed by having to do too many things. He cares about us, too. If time allows, discuss the priorities of Mary and Martha and the importance of maintaining our relationship with Christ before other activities.

As kids leave, give each a copy of "Time Management Tips" (Student Sheet 6) to refer to this week.

Your kids may not realize it, but their schools are generally a pretty good place to be—relatively speaking. A lot of kids in less developed countries would love to go to these schools that feature trained teachers, audiovisual materials, well-stocked libraries, and good food. Well, decent food. Okay, it's usually *edible*.

But any school can be a tough place to be Christian. Following Jesus just isn't cool (or "rad" or "bogus" or whatever your kids are calling it at the moment). That's understandable, because Christianity never was meant to be popular. It is right, just, true, compassionate, purposeful, and all the other things that make faith good—but it's not fashionable in most circles, even in some Christian schools.

So how do kids flesh out the Christian faith in an indifferent-to-hostile school? How do they show others what they've found in Christ? How do they *carefully* show they care?

In this session, work with kids to help them come to grips with what it means to be Christians in their schools. Challenge them. Understand them, too.

When It's
Tough
To Be a Christian

The Point	To help young people develop love and concern for non-Christians at school, and to begin showing that love by treating non-Christians with respect and telling them about Christ.
The Passages	Colossians 4:3-6; John 14:26-27; 16:33; Proverbs 16:7; Romans 12:18; Matthew 9:35-38
The Preparation	You'll need the following: • Small prizes (optional) • Pencils • Bibles • Chalk and chalkboard or markers and newsprint • Copies of "Bible-less Study" (Student Sheet 7) • Copies of "Wrong-Way Witnesses" skits (Student Sheet 8) and students to act them out

A Heavy Issue
Demonstrating the Challenge of Persuading Others

Before class, select a large book (dictionary, concordance, etc.) and weigh it on an accurate scale. As students arrive, ask them to examine the book and decide exactly how heavy it is (to the nearest pound), but don't give them a chance to weigh it. After everyone has had a chance to examine the book, divide the group into three (probably unequal) "camps" according to how much they think the book weighs.

Now comes the fun part. Challenge each camp to convince others to join them by getting them to agree on the book's weight. This may get a little noisy!

After a few minutes of persuasive discussion, use these questions to examine what happened.

For those who changed camps: Why did you switch?

For those who didn't budge: Why didn't you switch?

What problems did you have when trying to convert others to your way of thinking?

What problems occurred when you changed your mind?

What were the most effective arguments you used? The least effective?

How did it feel to be in a small (or large) camp?

Ask kids how these "camps" are like Christians and non-Christians at school.

Which camp (Christian or non-Christian) tries harder to influence the other?

What methods does each use?

Which camp do you think has an easier job?

Wrap up the exercise by revealing the true weight of the book. If you like, give small prizes to the group whose estimate was most nearly correct.

A Lion's Den?
Sharing the Difficulties of Being a Christian at School

Explain that in this session you'll be talking about how to relate to non-Christians at school—especially about how hard it can be to let them know the Good News about Christ. Get kids talking about the difficulties of being a Christian at school by asking them the following question.

Which of these Bible stories is most like your experience of being a Christian at school—and why?

1. Daniel in the Lion's Den (trapped and persecuted)

2. Nicodemus Talks to Jesus at Night (a secret believer)

3. Peter Betrays Jesus (letting the Lord down)

4. David and Goliath (always victorious)

5. Jonah and the "Whale" (wanting unbelievers to get the punishment they deserve)

Encourage all to answer, but avoid forcing participation. Summarize the discussion by noting whether most of your kids feel persecuted, pressured, pretending, or pleasant where non-Christian classmates are concerned. If some of your students attend Christian schools, ask them whether they think it's easier or harder to share their faith with kids in a Christian school than in a public school.

Pick a Person
Identifying Qualities that Help Us Influence Others fo Christ

School can be a tough place to be, especially for a Christian. But you have a choice: to let others at school decide how you act and think, or to influence them instead. Let's start thinking about how people influence each other for Christ. Who, other than the Lord, has had the greatest influence on your being a Christian (or being in church) today?

Share your own answer to the question. Then ask the person on your right to respond, and so on. Allow students to pass if they want to. Responses might include teachers, friends, ministers, youth workers, coaches, parents, etc. Challenge each student to identify what the influential person said or did that had such a profound effect.

The apostle Paul attracted a lot of people to God. Let's see how.

Paul's Way
Examining Paul's Model for Sharing Faith

Hand out copies of "Bible-less Study" (Student Sheet 7), so called because it doesn't require looking up the verses; they're printed on the sheet. For now, concentrate only on Part 1, "Between the Lines."

Tell students to read the lines from Colossians 4:3-6 and write what each line says to them about how Christians should share their faith. Then have them re-gather and share their ideas. Here are some possibilities, numbered by line:

1. You need others praying for you; pray for opportunities.
2. You want to draw people to Christ, not just to agreeing with you.
3. You need to know the basics of the Gospel and explain them in a way others can understand.
4. Your actions toward non-Christians speak at least as loudly as your words.
5. When you have a chance to share your faith, do something with it.
6. Take care that the way you talk draws people to Jesus instead of driving them away.
7. Don't just talk about superficial things.
8. Be prepared to answer non-Christians' questions.

Not Me!
Letting Scripture Answer Our Objections to Witnessing

Have kids look at "Multiple Matchup," Part 2 of Student Sheet 7. Explain that you're about to read several objections to sharing our faith. Kids should determine which passages offer guidance about each issue, then stand up and tell why.

Here are the statements and verses that might apply:

1. When people "witness," they usually seem to cause more conflict and anger than good. (Proverbs 16:7; Romans 12:18.)

2. I'm too afraid to stand up for my beliefs. (John 16:33; 14:26, 27.)

3. I wouldn't know what to say. (John 14:26, 27.)

4. Why should I witness, when all my friends are Christians? (Matthew 9:35-38.)

5. There are plenty of people witnessing already; I don't have to get involved. (Matthew 9:35-38.)

6. I don't care what happens to non-Christians; they deserve whatever they get. (Matthew 9:35-38.)

Ask kids what's hardest for them about the idea of sharing their faith. Have they ever tried to do it?

If you've tried witnessing at school, maybe it didn't work out exactly the way you'd planned. We're going to see a couple of examples of that now.

Wrong-Way Witnessing
Finding Ways to Witness by Laughing at Some Bad Examples

Before class, recruit four students to practice and perform the two skits found on "Wrong-Way Witnesses" (Student Sheet 8). Give them time to present their skits. Ask the following questions after each skit.

Was there anything good about this witnessing approach?

What was negative about it?

How do you think each character in the skit felt? How would you respond if you were on the receiving end of this approach?

What might cause a Christian to act this way?

What effect do you think this approach would have on kids in your school?

A Daydream
Envisioning Kids We Know Who Need God's Presence

Tell your kids that you want to spend the last few minutes of class being a bit more serious. You're going to close the class with a sort of daydream. Students should listen closely as you walk them through this exercise in imagination; if you like, you could have them close their eyes to help them concentrate.

Imagine that you are at school. You are between classes and most of your friends are walking by. Everyone seems happy.

Except one person. Someone you know, a person who's going through a tough time, stands across the hall from you. Picture him or her in your mind. Think about the person's first name or initials. (Pause to allow kids to picture this scene.)

As you watch this person, imagine that all of a sudden you see Jesus coming toward him. Jesus doesn't do or say much, but stays beside this person for a long time.

You walk over to the pair. Perhaps you touch your classmate on the shoulder. Perhaps you just lean against the wall.

You look on the opposite side of the hall and you see a large window. In the reflection you see Jesus, your classmate, and yourself. Then you turn away from the window and notice that just the two of you—your needy classmate and you—are in the hallway. You no longer see Jesus, but you know He's still there with you.

Think for a few moments about this person at school. Spend a while in silent prayer for him or her.

Ask God to help each student reach out to the one in the daydream. Ask Him to open the door for honest sharing and to give each group member strength to talk with that classmate. Thank God for His help.

What was your favorite class in high school?

What did you enjoy most about high school?

What are some of your fondest memories?

What would have made school even better?

What kept you from getting the most out of school?

What can you do during this hour or so to help your students get the most out of their high school years?

These are some questions you might want to ask yourself as you prepare this session. Since by law your kids have to go to school (unless they drop out, which is even worse), they might as well get as much out of it as they can. That doesn't just mean studying hard, making friends, and going to as many parties as possible. It means tasting the life Christ came to give us—the fullest kind of life possible (John 10:10).

The "abundant life" isn't just for adults, and it isn't just for Sundays. If you can help your kids see how Christ's presence changes life at school, you'll be helping them get a lot more out of their Mondays through Fridays.

You Might As Well Enjoy It

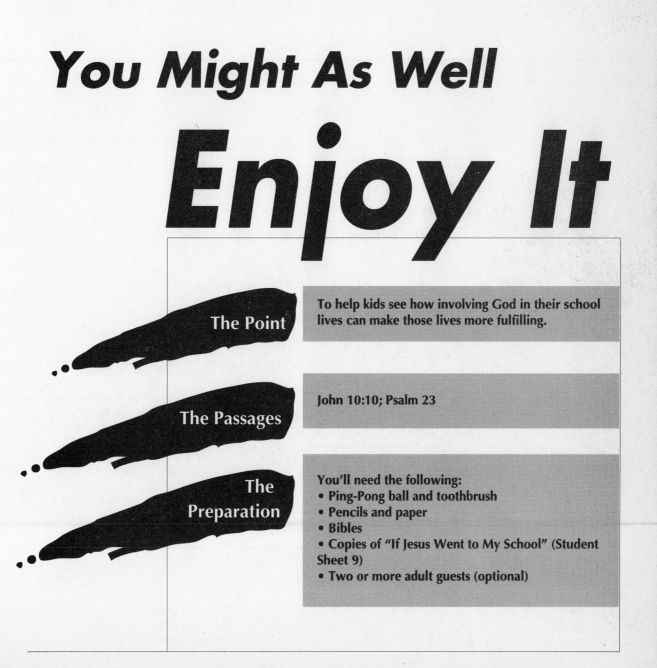

The Point — To help kids see how involving God in their school lives can make those lives more fulfilling.

The Passages — John 10:10; Psalm 23

The Preparation — You'll need the following:
- Ping-Pong ball and toothbrush
- Pencils and paper
- Bibles
- Copies of "If Jesus Went to My School" (Student Sheet 9)
- Two or more adult guests (optional)

Miniature Baseball
Showing How the Right Resources Affect Our Results

Announce that you're going to play baseball. Split the group into two teams. You can go outside if you like, but it's not necessary. That's because you're playing *miniature* baseball—using a Ping-Pong ball for a baseball and a toothbrush for a bat.

Play an inning or so of this game, adapting normal baseball rules to fit the equipment and space. Kids will probably find that they have to move in close to the batter, shrinking the whole game to a fraction of its normal size.

Then discuss the problems encountered—difficulty in hitting the ball, hard to pitch, etc. Ask whether kids prefer miniature baseball or the real thing. Most will probably choose the full-sized version. Use this activity to make a point with comments like these:

If we had the right equipment here to play real baseball, most of us wouldn't choose to play with a Ping-Pong ball and a toothbrush. We want the real thing, the full experience.

That's true of school, too. We want to get a lot out of it and even enjoy it—not just go through the motions.

Getting the most out of something requires using all the resources you've got. If you're a Christian, your relationship with Christ is your most important resource. Depending on Him can help you get the most out of school—not to mention the rest of life.

Let's hear some experiences of people who have discovered how true that is.

If Only . . .
Learning from the Lives of Former Students

Before the session, arrange to have two or more adults from your church visit the group. These guests should be prepared to answer the following questions:

When you went to school, did you like it or hate it? Why?

If you could travel back in time and go through school again, what would you do differently?

How could your relationship with Christ have helped you get more out of school?

If you're unable to locate guests, prepare to answer these questions from your own experience. As you or your guests prepare, consider how each of the following might have helped you in school: prayer, Bible reading, remembering that God was with you, being involved in a church youth group, and having some Christian friends. Let kids ask related questions of you or your guests if time allows.

The Great Life
Examining the Full Life That Jesus Gives

Have someone read John 10:10. Ask: **What do you think Jesus means when He promises that His followers can have "life. . . to the full"?** (Some possibilities: more meaning to life; peace about the future; concentrating on the important things; living the way God designed us to live; joy, etc.)

Point out that in the verses following John 10:10, Jesus described Himself as a shepherd. **Now let's look at another famous chapter of the Bible that talks about the Lord as a shepherd.**

Have kids turn to Psalm 23. Volunteers should read it aloud a verse at a time. After each verse, ask how Christ's role as shepherd leads to a better life for His sheep—His followers. Here are some possible answers, numbered by verse:

1. He makes sure we have all we need.
2. He gives us peace and rest.
3. He gives us new strength when we're worn out and helps us stay on the right moral path.
4. He stays with us, comforting and protecting us even in the most dangerous, emotionally hard times.
5. He protects us from enemies and gives us even more than we need.
6. He is good to us, loves us, never leaves us, and promises that we will live with Him forever.

Since we don't spend much of our time wandering around in meadows like sheep, we may wonder what the presence of Jesus has to do with school. Let's exercise our imaginations to find out.

Guess Who's Coming to School?
Imagining How Jesus Could Change Our School Lives

Pass out copies of "If Jesus Went to My School" (Student Sheet 9). Ask kids to write in each area, briefly describing how the people and relationships there might be different if Jesus were physically present every day.

After a few minutes, ask volunteers to share their thoughts with the rest of the group. You may wish to model such sharing by showing a worksheet you've filled out, based on your own school experiences. Avoid pressing for "right" answers; concentrate on the contrast between current attitudes at school and those Christ might exhibit—and the influence His example might have.

Point out that Christ *is* at school every day—not physically, but He's there. **If we remembered every day that Jesus goes to our school, how might that affect us in the areas on the worksheet? How could "taking Jesus to school" give us more of the full life He talked about?** (Answers will vary. If needed, suggest that kids adapt the principles from Psalm 23 to specific areas on their worksheets.)

A Psalm for School
Expressing Thanks for Christ's Presence at School

Have kids as a group, or in teams, paraphrase Psalm 23 in a way that shows how the Lord can guide, comfort, protect, and provide for them at school. Then ask them to read their psalm(s) aloud. Here's an example of what they might come up with:

"The Lord is my school Counselor; He provides all I need. He gives me a way to get to school; He leads me to pick the right classes; He helps me remember His presence even when I'm in the middle of a noisy school bus. He helps me say no to cheating so that people will know He is stronger than temptation.

"Even though I face a test that is worth a third of my grade, I will fear no evil, for You are with me; You remind me of what I've studied, and You keep my thoughts peaceful.

"You give me a place in the cafeteria and a couple of friends to sit with. You help me discover my interests by letting me play in the band or on the team or doing an experiment in chemistry class. I have so many opportunities that my schedule overflows.

"Surely Your goodness and love will follow me even after I graduate, and I will learn in the school of the Lord forever."

Close by breaking the group into pairs. Ask kids to pray for each other's most pressing needs at school. They may want to use their "If Jesus Went to My School" answers to help them think of prayer requests.

Temperature's Rising

Examine the following list of high-pressure items. How much influence do they place on you in school? Write down each item beside the thermometer at the point that best describes how much pressure it causes you.

Competition for Grades
School Band or Drama
Temptation to Cheat
Sports and Sporting Events
Peer Pressure
Lack of Christians
Competition for College
Violence or Intimidation
Tough Teacher
Amount of Homework
Rules and Administrators
Being New at School

School Survival Kit

You've got to survive somehow at school. How are you going to cope with the stress? Maybe you've got help you could call on, but hadn't really thought about how to use it.

Use the blanks below to name specific people and ideas that could help you handle school stress. Chances are that not all of them will apply to you. But for each that does, describe a specific class or other school activity or relationship this "resource" could help you handle this year.

An older brother or sister
How he or she might help

Someone to pray for you
How that might help

A teacher or coach
How he or she might help

A Bible verse
How it might help

A parent
How he or she might help

A friend
How he or she might help

Something about knowing Jesus
How He might help

Part of a song you like
How it might help

Someone at church
How he or she might help

The example of someone in the Bible
How it might help

Remembering a time God helped you before
How that might help

Cutting out an extracurricular activity
How that might help

Teacher Report Card

C B+ A-

F

What overall letter grade would you give your teachers? _____

Now check the qualities that apply:

Quality	Good Teachers Demonstrate This	Mine Demonstrate This
Strict	❏	❏
Demanding	❏	❏
Creative	❏	❏
Friendly	❏	❏
Competent	❏	❏
Organized	❏	❏
Interesting	❏	❏
Fair	❏	❏
Knowledgeable	❏	❏
Understanding	❏	❏

D-

D- C+

A- C D- B+

B+ F

Cheating Test

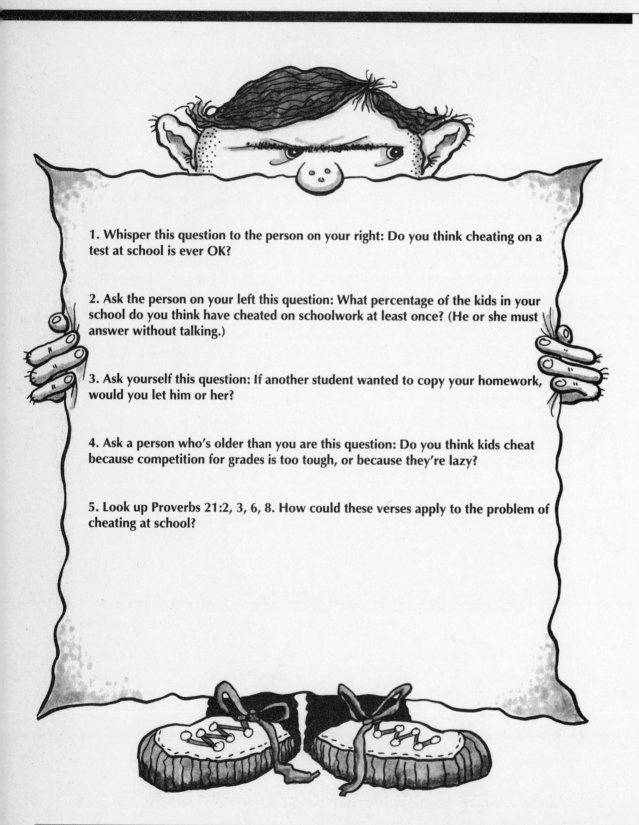

1. Whisper this question to the person on your right: Do you think cheating on a test at school is ever OK?

2. Ask the person on your left this question: What percentage of the kids in your school do you think have cheated on schoolwork at least once? (He or she must answer without talking.)

3. Ask yourself this question: If another student wanted to copy your homework, would you let him or her?

4. Ask a person who's older than you are this question: Do you think kids cheat because competition for grades is too tough, or because they're lazy?

5. Look up Proverbs 21:2, 3, 6, 8. How could these verses apply to the problem of cheating at school?

Letter to Larry

Larry's grades are slipping. He's a good student, but the last report card did little to reflect that. He pulled a "D" in physics and a "D" in world history. History! That used to be his favorite subject. He even considered being a history major in college. Looks like he'd better improve his grades, or his chances for college will be history.

He never seems to have time anymore. He's dating Sherry, which seems to take a lot of hours. Then there's afternoon tennis practice. Larry had made the number one spot on the tennis team, but doubts he can keep it for a whole year. He was also elected president of the youth group, and the youth director seems to have him attending more meetings than the President of the United States goes to. In fact, Larry seems to be gone on a weekend planning retreat once a month. Add to these the little things like sleeping, eating, mowing the lawn, and breathing—and you can see that Larry has a packed schedule.

You're concerned. Not nosy, just concerned. Take a moment and write Larry a note, giving him your best advice. Try to include some of the information discussed today. Larry couldn't be here to get your advice in person; he's gone on another youth retreat.

Dear Larry,

Time Management Tips

Twelve Sensible Suggestions on How to Accomplish What You Have to Do in the Time You Have

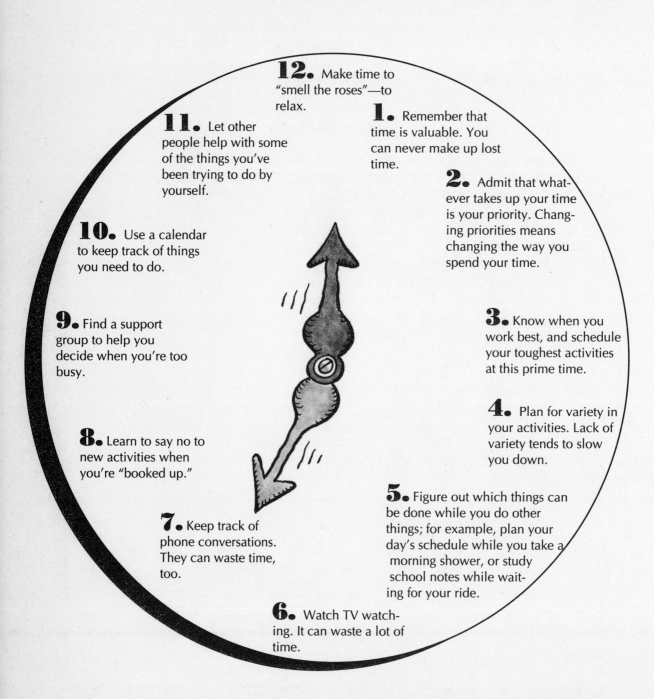

12. Make time to "smell the roses"—to relax.

11. Let other people help with some of the things you've been trying to do by yourself.

10. Use a calendar to keep track of things you need to do.

9. Find a support group to help you decide when you're too busy.

8. Learn to say no to new activities when you're "booked up."

7. Keep track of phone conversations. They can waste time, too.

6. Watch TV watching. It can waste a lot of time.

1. Remember that time is valuable. You can never make up lost time.

2. Admit that whatever takes up your time is your priority. Changing priorities means changing the way you spend your time.

3. Know when you work best, and schedule your toughest activities at this prime time.

4. Plan for variety in your activities. Lack of variety tends to slow you down.

5. Figure out which things can be done while you do other things; for example, plan your day's schedule while you take a morning shower, or study school notes while waiting for your ride.

Bible-less Study

P art 1: Between the Lines

Examine the lines of Scripture to find principles Paul used in his efforts to tell others about Christ. In your own words, write what each line has to say about how we should share our faith.

"¹And pray for us, too, that God may open a door for our message,

²so that we may proclaim the mystery of Christ, for which I am in chains.

³Pray that I may proclaim it clearly, as I should.

⁴Be wise in the way you act toward outsiders;

⁵make the most of every opportunity.

⁶Let your conversation be always full of grace,

⁷seasoned with salt,

⁸so that you may know how to answer everyone."

—*Colossians 4:3-6*

P art 2: Multiple Matchup

Wait for instructions on this one!

a. **John 16:33:** "I have told you these things, so that in me you may have peace. In this world you will have trouble. But take heart! I have overcome the world."

b. **Proverbs 16:7:** "When a man's ways are pleasing to the Lord, he makes even his enemies live at peace with him."

c. **Romans 12:18:** "If it is possible, as far as it depends on you, live at peace with everyone. Do not take revenge, my friends, but leave room for God's wrath, for it is written: 'It is mine to avenge; I will repay,' says the Lord."

d. **Matthew 9:35-38:** "Jesus went through all the towns and villages, teaching in their synagogues, preaching the good news of the kingdom and healing every disease and sickness. When he saw the crowds, he had compassion on them, because they were harassed and helpless, like sheep without a shepherd. Then he said to his disciples, 'The harvest is plentiful but the workers are few. Ask the Lord of the harvest, therefore, to send out workers into his harvest field.'"

e. **John 14:26, 27:** "But the Counselor, the Holy Spirit, whom the Father will send in my name, will teach you all things and will remind you of everything I have said to you. Peace I leave with you; my peace I give you. I do not give to you as the world gives. Do not let your hearts be troubled and do not be afraid."

Wrong-Way Witnesses

SKIT 1: *Incident in the Hall at School*

JIM: Excuse me, young lady. I'm looking for the office. Can you...

TINA: You're lost, huh? My name is Tina *(extends hand)*. I can show you the way.

JIM: Thanks, Tina. My name's Jim. You don't have to show me. If you could just give me directions—

TINA: Small is the gate and narrow the road that leads to life, and only a few will find it.

JIM: Gate? There's no gate in this building.

TINA: It is easier for a camel to go through the eye of a needle than it is to enter the Kingdom of Heaven. Are you prepared to enter the Kingdom of Heaven, Jim?

JIM: Sure, but first I'd like to find the school office.

TINA: Not everyone who says, "Lord, Lord" will enter the Kingdom of Heaven, but only he who does the will of my Father who is in Heaven. How do you know that you will enter the Kingdom of Heaven, Jim?

JIM: Because I'm doing God's will. Right now His will is for me to be in the office. I think I'd better find it on my own.

TINA: Watch out! You do not know when the time will come. It's like a man going away: He leaves his house in charge of his servants, each with his assigned task, and tells the one at the door to keep watch.

JIM: My house is fine. I have a security system.

TINA: Tell me, Jim: Why are you here?

JIM: I'm new in town. I wanted to drop by to introduce myself to the principal. I'm the new youth minister at the church down the street. Nice talking with you! *(He walks away.)*

SKIT 2: *Another Incident in the Hall at School*

KRIS: Hey, Tom! Becky said you went on a church youth retreat with her last week. That true?

TOM: *(Panics)* Uh. . . I don't remember.

KRIS: You don't remember?

TOM: Last week was a long time ago, you know.

KRIS: Tom—this is Tuesday.

TOM: Yeah. You're right. I went with them. Just to meet some girls, though.

KRIS: I wish I could have gone. I've been wondering about that stuff lately.

TOM: You have?

KRIS: Yeah. You know, all that stuff we learned as kids in Sunday School. It didn't answer all my questions.

TOM: So, uh, why don't you talk to a minister or something?

KRIS: I kinda thought it would be easier to talk to you. I heard somebody say you were a Christian.

TOM: Uh-oh. . . . uh . . . I've gotta run. I've got to—uh—watch an old TV rerun of *McHale's Navy* for—uh—physics class. Yeah, that's it.

KRIS: Oh. Maybe we can talk later?

TOM: Naw, you'd better find a minister. Goodbye—and good luck!

If Jesus Went To My School

What might your school be like if Jesus regularly attended it—physically, in Person? Jot down a few ideas about how each of the following areas (and the people and relationships in them) might change if Jesus were known to spend a lot of time there.

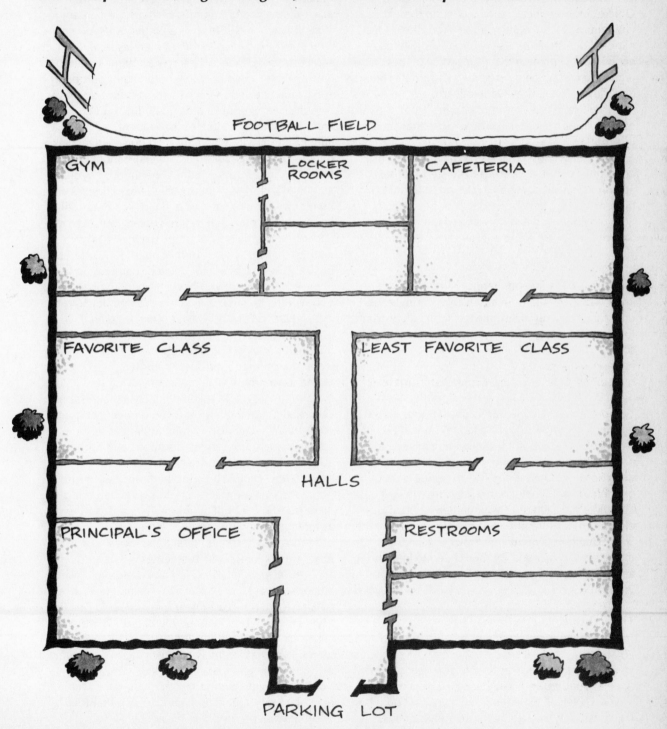

How to Talk to Kids about Being Male and Female

by Tim Stafford

You have one huge advantage when you talk to kids about their sexuality: they're interested. Unlike some subjects that you have to dress up with gimmicks, sexuality can be—must be—handled in a straightforward way. Even when kids act bored, even when they act as though they know it all, you can be pretty sure it's just a front. They don't know it all. They want to learn.

You're in a very important role. Think for a minute about the others who talk to teenagers on this topic:

• Television, movies, and magazines, which constantly stimulate desire and suggest that sexual activity is part of being a sophisticated, fulfilled person.

• Schools, most of which provide biological information but not much else.

• Parents.

• Other kids.

And that's the whole list! Many kids have no adult who can talk to them sensibly, caringly, yet unemotionally about sex and sexuality. They aren't looking for biology lessons, by and large, though some may be. They want to know what love is, how sex fits with it, how to find lasting love, what's right and wrong with sexual activity—and why.

While writing a column on love and sex in *Campus Life* magazine for the past 15 years, I've answered just about every question an adolescent can think of. You don't have that advantage. You'll probably be thinking on your feet sometimes, and that can be scary. But don't worry about it. You may not be able to answer every question to the complete satisfaction of your audience; I can't, either. I'm not sure anyone can.

But the way you give answers is just as important as what you say. Kids need to hear an adult they trust giving them a Christian point of view on sex.

Tips to Remember

Here are a few concerns to keep in mind as you talk:

• *Try to remember the broad range of experience in your group.* Most kids won't open up about their own sexual experiences in a group. You'll be left guessing what's going through their minds.

The temptation is to assume one extreme or the other. You can think, *These are nice church kids (and so young!) that they can't have had any sexual experience.* Or you can think, *Kids today are so messed up, I have to talk to them as sexual sophisticates.* Either of these assumptions would be a mistake, for it would leave out a major portion of your audience.

In most groups of kids (including church kids, and including those in their early teens) a significant minority will have had intercourse at least once. The average for all teenagers is about one in four. As you talk, assume that one in four of your audience is thinking about specific experiences and relationships he or she has been in—and may still be in. On the other hand, three out of four have not had sex, and so feel "out of it," naive. You don't want to make them feel further out of it by addressing only the sexually experienced. Rather, you want to encourage those who haven't been involved in sex with the fact that they're on the right track.

• *Answer every question you're asked.* I usually find it best to take written questions, passing out pieces of paper, and asking each person to write a question. (If kids use their own paper, or only a few of them write questions, it's too easy for them to identify who asked what.) Many questions get asked anonymously that would never get asked out loud. You can also usually arrange it so there's a chance for you to screen questions and think about them before you try to answer them.

Often you'll get some smart-aleck questions from kids who are trying to rattle you. Don't throw these questions out. If at all possible, answer them as though they were serious. That establishes a tone of seriousness and openness. It lets kids know that there are no "off-limits" subjects.

• *Be specific.* If you feel uncomfortable using anatomical terms or words like sexual intercourse, making love, or orgasm, you might want to practice saying them in private until you can do it without your ears turning red. It's not that you need to pretend you're extremely sophisticated. It's just that if you seem at ease, it will help kids feel at ease. You'll communicate to them that you're relaxed enough to talk specifically about sex, rather than wishing you could skip the subject entirely.

• *Be personal and vulnerable.* You don't need to come off as a person who knows all the answers or has never made a mistake. On the contrary, the more vulnerable you can be the better.

Let me use myself as an example. I believe that admitting my own struggles has helped kids as much as my Bible-based comments. It tells them that I really understand their feelings, and that normal people struggle with issues like masturbation and maintaining sexual control when dating.

Though kids may seem terribly sophisticated, they're usually aware of their lack of experience. They're open to an adult perspective, especially if it's not all theory but seems to be based on experiences they can relate to.

• *Be idealistic.* Sex is a great gift from God, and kids know it. Don't spend your time trying to scare them to death. AIDS, herpes, premarital pregnancy, and other problems associated with sex are frightening. They should be talked about realistically. But you don't want to emphasize them so much that the goodness of God's gift gets obscured.

I doubt fear is the most effective motive for good behavior anyway. Idealism is better. If you can communicate the goodness of relationships that are genuinely pure in heart, if you can communicate the attractiveness of a marriage in which two people don't start off with a history of past partners, if you can show how beautifully God provides for the needs of men and women in marriage, then you give kids something to hope for and aim for. If you yourself are sexually satisfied, let them know!

It would also be helpful to offer some idealism about singleness. Our society treats it like a disease. It's not. Many people live satisfied, graceful single lives. They need to be held up as models. After all, both Jesus and the apostle Paul led the way for this style of life.

• *Have some resource books available.* You can't cover everything about sexuality in five weeks. But if you make some books readily available, kids will be able to fill in the gaps. You may even want to ask volunteers to do book reports. A kid's recommendation might go further than yours. And at least *one* kid will read the book in order to report on it.

Christian bookstores have some excellent material available. If you can get money from the church budget to buy enough copies, they'll probably get read. (Another option: Ask parents for the money.) If you just recommend books but don't provide them, most kids won't make the effort to get to the bookstore.

Talking to kids about being male and female may not be easy, but it's worthwhile. Your students may not remember exactly what you tell them. But they will remember you, the way you talked to them—and the main points you made.

Tim Stafford is senior writer for Christianity Today *magazine. He also answers kids' questions in his popular* Campus Life *column, "Love, Sex, and the Whole Person." His books include* Knowing the Face of God *(Zondervan).*

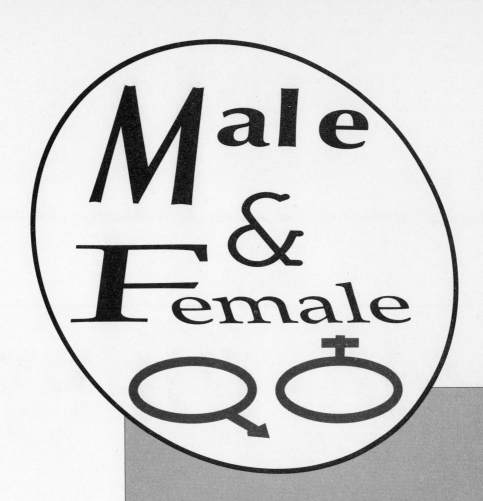

by Sandy Larsen

Sandy Larsen is a freelance writer who lives in Ashland, Wisconsin. By herself or with her husband Dale she has authored about two dozen Bible study courses for teens, plus others for adults. Besides teaching teenagers in Sunday School, she finds time for canoeing, camping, and working with two theatre groups.

"If I don't have sex by the time I'm out of high school, I'll be weird! People will wonder about me!"

It isn't only the "bad" kids who feel the pressure now; all young people feel it, even Christians. From peers, TV, and movies they get the message that being sexually active is the only normal way for a teenager to go. Even the AIDS epidemic brings recommendations for "safe" teen sex, not abstinence. No wonder kids question whether abstinence is healthy—or even possible!

In this session and the four to follow, you'll help your young people see God's perspective on sex. They'll discuss His alternatives to the world's misuse of His gift. Kids will probably expect lists of "don'ts" when the subject is announced; you can surprise them by keeping the mood positive and hopeful.

It's Good, But It's Not Everything

The Point
To help kids understand God's perspective on their sexuality, to contrast that with attitudes they and those around them may hold, and to encourage kids to use God's view as the ultimate standard.

The Passages
Genesis 1:27, 28, 31; 2:21-25; Proverbs 6:20, 27-29; Hebrews 13:4

The Preparation
You'll need the following:
• Copies of "Your Order, Please" (Student Sheet 10)
• Pencils
• Bibles
• Copies of "A Sure Way for Scorched Feet" (Student Sheet 11)

It's Everywhere!
Experiencing the Power of Obsessive Thoughts

As students come in, tell them: **For the next minute I want each of you not to think about the walls in this room.**

Keep track of time. At the end of one minute, ask students how well they did. They undoubtedly found it very difficult, if not impossible, to not think about the walls once the walls had been pointed out to them. Some may have been able to divert their thoughts by deliberately looking at and concentrating on something else—but it's unlikely that even they were able to block fleeting thoughts completely.

Make the application to teen sexuality by saying something along these lines:

The whole issue of being male or female is something like thinking about the walls of this room. Sexuality is here, all around you. Sometimes it seems to be everywhere you look. The more you try not to think about these walls, the more conscious of them you are. The same is true of your sexuality—if you try to keep your thoughts "pure" by denying or ignoring your sexual feelings, you'll probably wind up obsessed with sexual thoughts to the point of feeling guilty.

We should feel free to honestly recognize that we're males and females and that this is an important part of us. But it's only part. Just like there are other important things in this room besides the walls, there are other good things in life besides our sexual feelings.

Pulling Rank
Exploring the Relative Importance of Sex and Sexuality

Hand out "Your Order, Please" (Student Sheet 10). Give students time to think about these lists and honestly rank the items in order of importance. If volunteers want to share the results, discuss; otherwise keep the answers confidential.

Whether or not answers are shared, discuss the exercise in a general way with questions like these:

Was it hard to put these items in order? Why or why not?

How did you decide which things were most important to you?

Do you think your answers are like or unlike those most kids at school would give? Why?

What do your answers tell you about how important sex and sexuality are?

Do you think your answers might change in a few years? Why or why not?

If sex isn't the most important thing in the world, why does it sometimes seem that important to many people? (Reasons could include the influence of our hormones, loneliness, peer pressure, stimulation from TV commercials and other sources, a "now or never" feeling, and wanting to have power over other people.)

Observe that while we shouldn't deny our sexuality, our maleness or femaleness is not the most important thing about us. In many situations it makes little or no difference. And if we concentrate only on fulfilling our sexual desires, we'll miss most of what life has to offer. Whether we're male or female, the most important thing about us is that we're human beings made in God's image.

Very, Very Good
Remembering That God Created Sexual People

Have a couple of kids read aloud Genesis 1:27, 28, 31 and 2:21-25. Discuss along these lines:

What did God call "very good"? (Everything He had made, including male and female people and the responsibilities and blessings he had given them.)

Do all people today think sexuality is "very good"? (No. Some think it's good; some think it's evil or dirty; some think it's only "good" in the sense that they get some physical thrills out of it, not in the sense that God approves of it.)

Why do you think people sometimes have the attitude that our sexuality is bad rather than very good? (Some possibilities: They may think sexual desires are so difficult to control that sexuality itself must be bad; they might feel embarrassed about the human body; they might feel shame over not following God's guidelines for sex; they might think that since sex is private, it's bad; they may never have heard people talk about it outside of dirty jokes.)

Point out that since God's proclamation of "very good" in Genesis 1:31, sin has entered the world and perverted all of human life, including our sexual attitudes and practices. Yet even sin hasn't been able to destroy the goodness of our sexuality which God created. Used as He wants, it's still "very good."

Who did God tell to be fruitful, subdue the earth, and rule over the animals? The man or the woman? (Both.) **What's the feeling or mood of the passage about the creation of woman (2:21-25)?** (Some possibilities: intimacy, joy, togetherness, love, openness. There's no sense of domination or slavery or competition between the sexes as God puts the woman and man together.)

Being male and female is a gift from God. If somebody gives you a gift, how can you find out the best way to use it? (Ask the person who gave it to you; consult the instructions that came with it; talk to the one who invented it or someone who already has such a gift.) **How can we find out how to use the very good gift of sexuality God has given us?** (Find out from Him—especially through the Bible—how He wants it to be used. That's true of sex, food, the earth's resources, intelligence, money, or any other gift.)

Scorched Feet
Contrasting God's Sexual Standards with the World's

All God's gifts to us are good, but sin has a way of warping them and us. Sin puts trouble into all our personal relationships, including the sexual one.

Hand out "A Sure Way for Scorched Feet" (Student Sheet 11). Let students work individually on reading the verses and answering the question. Follow up with questions like these:

What positive thing about sex and marriage does the Hebrews verse have to say? (A healthy sexual relationship in marriage, symbolized by the bed, is pure and therefore approved by God. That special relationship is worth honoring. You might say that God's idea of "safe sex" is strictly within marriage.)

If you took a survey at school on kids' reactions to all these verses, what do you think most of them would say? (Some would probably laugh or call the Bible's attitudes old-fashioned.) **How do TV and movie attitudes compare with these verses?** (Hollywood tends to approve of premarital and extramarital sex, even implying that it's better than sex in marriage. And the idea of taking advice from your parents isn't popular on the screen, either.)

God's standards for sex are still alive and well, even though people ignore or laugh at them—and at Him. Because He loves us, He makes plans that are in our best interest. Going against His instructions brings built-in trouble—not because He wants us to be miserable, but because He understands sexuality far better than anyone else does.

Have students, working in small groups, label the "coals" on their worksheets. Some possible labels for the "coals": guilt, fear of discovery, bad memories later, pregnancy, abortion, revenge (by the adulterer's spouse), damaged relationship with God, AIDS and other diseases, emotional pain when the relationship ends, and damage to future relationships.

Sum up the message of the student sheet this way: **There are consequences for going against God's purposes in any part of life, and that includes sex. Some consequences are long-term and some short-term. But they're still there, no matter how much people try to deny or ignore them.**

Going by the Book
Celebrating the Rewards of Obeying God

Step 5

Now that you've looked at the "hot coals" of being burned by disobedience, focus on the rewards of obeying—living by God's sexual standards.
What are some positive results of obeying the following directions?
1. On a hair dryer: "Do not use this appliance in the bathtub or when standing in water." (Getting dry hair—and living to tell about it.)
2. On a can of oven cleaner: "Keep out of reach of children." (Peace of mind, safe children.)
3. On a car dashboard: "Use unleaded fuel only." (Less air pollution, undamaged engine.)
4. On a prescription: "For external use only." (Getting over an illness, feeling better, not making yourself sicker.)
5. At a fast-food restaurant: "Place order here." (Getting your food, saving time by not waiting in the wrong line.)
Following directions can make us glad we did. Obeying isn't just avoiding bad results; it's getting good results, too. What are some good results of obeying God with our sexual attitudes and behavior?
(Kids will probably need a few moments to ponder this. Suggest that they think about the "flip side" of the hot coals mentioned earlier. Answers might include learning self-control; being confident we're living as God wants; building our relationship with Him; having better relationships with people; living for God and others rather than solely for ourselves; getting to know the opposite sex as more than sex objects; finding out we're stronger than we thought we were; having the joy of going into marriage without guilt or regrets; having the freedom to do other things; staying physically healthy.)

Have kids sum up today's findings: There's more to us than our sexuality; God made us sexual beings; our sexuality is an important part of us; it's good, but it isn't everything in life; we find our greatest happiness obeying God in everything, and that includes sex.

Close the session on a positive note, thanking God for making us male and female and for His help in following His plans for us.

"John and Susan walk home from school together every day and ride around together in John's car. She's over at his house all the time, or else he's over at her house. Sure, they say they're 'just friends,' but there's got to be something going on between them!"

Can a girl and guy be friends—good friends, close friends—without romantic involvement? Of course they can. But some people don't see it. They think if you spend much time with a member of the opposite sex, you must be going together. Otherwise why would you bother to be together? Such an attitude can press girls and guys to relate sexually or not at all.

You can help your teens see beyond this narrow view of male-female relationships. They can learn to value each other for the people they are, and enjoy giving and receiving from each other without romantic involvement.

More Than a
Date

The Point

To help students recognize the value of members of the opposite sex, based on God's view, and to help them respect and develop friendships with the opposite sex.

The Passages

Galatians 3:26-28; Luke 8:1-3; John 11:1-5; Acts 16:13-15

The Preparation

You'll need the following:
• Posterboard (one sheet)
• Markers (at least one per student)
• Pair of scissors
• Tape
• Paper, pencils
• Small, shareable prize
• Bibles
• Copies of "Friends Unafraid" (Student Sheet 12)
• Copies of "The Buddy System" (Student Sheet 13)

Form-A-Friend
Identifying Qualities that Apply to Both Sexes

Give students one sheet of posterboard. Have them elect a group member to draw a large cartoon outline of a person. The artist should try not to make the person look male or female. Have another student cut out the drawing.

Then explain: **This is the outline of your ideal friend. Now you're going to fill it in with the qualities that make a good friend.**

Divide the group into pairs or threes—preferably mixed-gender teams. Have a student cut the "person" into several pieces—one piece for each pair or group of three—and give one piece to each small group. Hand out colored markers. Instruct the small groups: **Brainstorm qualities that you think make a person a good friend. Decide on one quality which you think is most important, and write it on your "piece" of the ideal friend.**

When groups have finished, give them tape and have them fasten the pieces of their "friend" back together. Read what's written on each section to get a fuller picture of an ideal friend. If a quality is repeated on several sections, that tells you what your students think is especially important in friendship. Discuss these qualities and others which make a good friend.

Ask: **Does this friend have to be the same sex that you are? Or could it be someone of the opposite sex?** (It's likely that most of the qualities of friendship could be had by a person of either sex. Some students may say they are more comfortable sharing very personal things with someone of the same sex. The point is that it's possible to have good friends of the opposite sex.)

Nothing in Common?
Discovering Foundations for Opposite-sex Friendships

Have the pairs or threes (which should mix guys and girls if at all possible) scatter to different parts of the room. Give each group a sheet of paper and a pencil.

Explain: **Some people think friendship with the opposite sex is impossible because guys and girls have nothing in common. In your groups, take the next 60 seconds to come up with everything you can that your group members have in common. This includes big things like interests and beliefs—and little things like living in the same town and having the same number of noses!**

The group that comes up with the most things in a minute wins. Award a small, shareable prize (like a bag of peanuts) to the winning group. Discuss some of the things kids have in common regardless of gender, especially those that could help to form the basis for a friendship.

Just Friends
Confronting Barriers to Opposite-sex Friendships

One reason we tend not to make friends with people of the opposite sex is that we're afraid somebody will say, "Hey, look who's got a sweetheart!" What are some other reasons?

As needed, supplement kids' answers with this list:
1. We're not used to being around the opposite sex.

2. We think guys and girls have nothing in common.

3. We think the opposite sex is only good for romance or sexual activity.

4. The guy or girl might think we're trying to "put the moves on" and reject us.

5. He or she might want romance but we want friendship.

6. We feel peer pressure to get a boyfriend or girlfriend.

7. We or our parents might fear friendship would lead to sexual involvement.

8. Others might think we couldn't make friends with those of our own sex.

9. Others might think we were "gay" because we have too much in common with the opposite sex.

Suppose you'd like to be "just friends" with a member of the opposite sex. You don't have any romantic intentions. How can you keep the guy or girl from getting the wrong idea? (Advice will vary. One possibility: Be honest from the start. You don't have to make a speech; simply saying that you want to be "just friends" can cool off romantic expectations.)

How can you keep others from getting the wrong idea? (Maybe you can't. But you can tell them honestly what's going on, and in time they may accept your new friendship.)

Is it worth the risk to be friends with people of the opposite sex? Some very important people in the Bible thought so, as we'll see next.

Friends Unafraid
Examining Opposite-Sex Friendships in the Bible

Step 4

Hand out "Friends Unafraid" (Student Sheet 12). Keeping the same small groups, have students work on the Bible study together. Discuss their responses along the following lines.

Luke 8:1-3: **Who traveled with Jesus? How many were men? How many were women?** (The 12 disciples were men; three women are named, and there were "many others." Both the men and the women were an important part of Jesus' life and ministry.) **What rumors might Jesus' enemies have spread about Him and His companions?** (We can just hear the accusations of wrong motives and immorality. Jesus, the male disciples, and these women willingly took the risk of "what people might think" for the sake of their commitment to one another.)

John 11:1-5: **What does this Scripture tell you about the kind of friendships Jesus formed?** (He was close to the man *and* the women in this household. He could have been friends with Lazarus and ignored the sisters, but He chose to include the women also.)

Acts 16:13-15: **When the missionaries discovered only women at the place of prayer, what might they have done to fit in with the custom of the day?** (Gone somewhere else.) **What did they do instead?** (Sat down and shared the Gospel with them.) **With what results?** (Lydia, an influential woman, was saved, along with the rest of her household. The missionaries went to stay with her, and her home became a center for their ministry. She took risks by being associated with them, but she was willing to do that for Christ.)

Are Christians Sexless?
Seeing That Christ Transcends Gender Lines

Read Galatians 3:26-28 together. **This says there is neither male nor female. But we look around and it's obvious that each of us is either male or female! The Bible certainly doesn't mean we become sexless if we become Christians. What do you think Paul meant by this?**

Help kids see the context: Human differences are made unimportant in Christ. The meaning is clarified in Paul's further statement, "You are all one in Christ Jesus." Christ brings unity where we find cause for division. Males and females have equal standing in Christ, equal access to Him, equal value. Neither sex can lord it over the other, or feel inferior to the other.

Once you realize that Christ died for a particular person of the opposite sex, how does that change the way you see that person? (Possible answer: You see that person not as a sex object or an incomprehensible mystery or a pain in the neck, but as someone you can accept as Christ accepts—valuable in his or her own right, and valuable as much more than a potential date.)

Friendship Possibilities
Staying Open to Opposite-sex Friendships

Hand out Student Sheet 13, "The Buddy System." Have kids check off their answers. This exercise is light-hearted, but there is "meat" on the bones of the questions. Discuss how the possibilities under each statement reflect various ways of valuing or de-valuing the opposite sex.

Maybe this quiz will keep us thinking about having better friendships with the opposite sex. We can help each other, too. When we see a girl and guy acting friendly toward one another, we don't have to play matchmaker or jump to conclusions. Let's let people be free to enjoy each other's company without pressuring them about romance or sex. And let's enjoy each other's company as one in Christ.

"If God wants me to wait until marriage, why does He put all these feelings into me now? Does He expect me to go crazy for 10 or 15 years waiting for the right person to come along?"

Young Christians ask these pain-filled questions with good reason. And they aren't getting any help from peers who see sexual activity as a "given."

What can you tell your kids? "It's worth the wait—and God is there, waiting with you." This session is designed to help you get that message across.

The Waiting Game

The Point

To help teens understand God's directions to wait for sexual activity until marriage, and to help them deal with the frustration that waiting can bring.

The Passages

Romans 8:18-28; Exodus 20:14; Matthew 15:19; I Corinthians 6:18-20; Galatians 5:19; Ephesians 5:3; Colossians 3:5; I Thessalonians 4:3

The Preparation

You'll need the following:
• Calculator
• Bibles
• Pencils
• Copies of "Worth Waiting For?" (Student Sheet 14)
• Copies of "Regretfully Yours" (Student Sheet 15)

What's Worth The Wait?
Evaluating Our Willingness to Wait for Things We Want

Hand out Student Sheet 14, "Worth Waiting For?" Have students write their answers individually. As you discuss the results, note which items on the list are seen as only worth waiting a few minutes for, or maybe not at all. For others, kids might wait years, even forever. In many cases you may get the answer, "It depends"—on how much the concert tickets cost, for example. Or it depends on whether the same thing is available somewhere else.

In general, the more you value something, and the more important it is to you, the longer you will wait for it.

Call special attention to students' answers for "The right person to marry." How much do they value the right person, based on how long they are willing to wait for him or her?

Observe that if something isn't worth waiting for, we generally think it isn't very important. While we're waiting, we think it's torture. But some positive work is being done on us, inside, while we wait.

What are some good things that happen to us when we have to wait for something? (Possible answers: We learn patience; we get stronger; we find out that we survive even without the thing we're waiting for; we begin to trust God because He's in control and knows what's best for us; we have time to examine our values; we find out what's really important to us; we might even change our minds about what we want.)

Not Yet!
Understanding God's Instructions to Wait

Have a student read Exodus 20:14, the seventh commandment.

The Scripture we've just read prohibits adultery—sex with another person's spouse. But what if neither person is married? (The Bible's message is still the same. Sex without marriage is identified as a sin with an ugly name: fornication, a word often translated "sexual immorality" in the New International Version.)

Have students read the following Scriptures, each of which includes the word for fornication: Matthew 15:19; I Corinthians 6:18-20; Galatians 5:19; Ephesians 5:3; Colossians 3:5; I Thessalonians 4:3.

God leaves no doubt in His Word that sexual intercourse belongs only in marriage—not before it, not outside it. But why command us to wait? Does He just want to spoil our fun?

Give kids time to think and talk about this. As needed, point out that in telling us to wait, God protects the full sexual expression of ourselves by putting it in a context of loving commitment. Sex is meant to express the lifelong love of two people; outside of that, it is an emotional H-bomb. We can't make ourselves that vulnerable to another person—physically, emotionally, mentally, spiritually—and then walk away (or worse, be walked away from) as though it made no difference.

The same is true of couples who marry with the escape valve of divorce in mind; they are often surprised at how emotionally devastated they are when the relationship ends. The marriage license is not magic; the commitment in marriage is what counts.

Counting The Days
Seeing How Our Attitudes Affect Waiting

Let's pick a number out of the air and say you're going to get married in ten years. If you're going to obey God's plan and purposes for your sexuality, you're going to have to wait until then to have sex.

Help the group use a calculator, pencil, and paper to break ten years down into months, weeks, days, hours, minutes, and seconds. To make the calculating a little easier, don't take leap years into account. (Ten years equal 120 months; 520 weeks; 3,650 days; 87,600 hours; 5,256,000 minutes; 315,360,000 seconds.)

When you figure out these astronomical numbers, the wait looks impossible! Suppose you went around repeating these figures to yourself all the time, as in "I've got 4,292,660 minutes to go . . . I've got 4,292,659 minutes to go . . ." You'd go crazy! All you'd think about is what you couldn't have yet.

What we concentrate on has a lot to do with how difficult waiting gets. Yet even with the best attitude, waiting is difficult. Waiting for something good involves suffering while we don't have it.

While You Wait
Learning to Wait with Hope

Have kids take turns reading Romans 8:18-28 aloud. Explain that this Scripture is not specifically about sex; it is about the suffering caused by waiting for what we strongly desire but don't have. It certainly applies to Christian kids who are struggling with their sexual desires and trying to stay pure.

What attitude does Paul take here toward suffering? (It's difficult, but worth it when we're waiting to see what God will do.)

What are we waiting for? (In this passage the emphasis is on waiting for God's final victory over sin, which will happen at the return of Christ. Then our bodies will be made new, and all the old results of sin will be done away with. That's the ultimate thing we're waiting for. All the other things in between are temporary, including sex. That's good to keep in mind. Even if we marry and sex is ours, there will still be suffering and waiting because sin will be in the world until Christ returns.)

How would you define "hope?" (Students will give various answers. As needed, explain that we sometimes use the word "hope" to mean "wishful thinking," as in "I hope tomorrow's game doesn't get rained out." But the Biblical view of "hope" is much stronger and surer than that. It means a confident expectation based on God's goodness and faithfulness.)

Can you experience hope without waiting? (No, because hope involves not yet having something you want—in other words, going without it and waiting for it.)

Be sure to acknowledge that not everyone wants to get married. Some prefer to remain single, a choice Paul thought was a good idea. And some who hope for marriage don't find that hope realized. The ban on fornication holds for them, too.

God lets some of His people remain single. What does this Scripture say to them? (Our hope is in the Lord and in His best purposes for us. If He wants us to be single, He can give us the grace to live that way—or to live with another imperfect human being if we get married.)

How could verses 26-28 help a person who wants to wait until marriage but is having trouble resisting his or her sexual urges? (They show that God is our Friend in the struggle to stay pure. They tell us we can rely on God's Spirit to help us where we're weak. Even when we're too confused or emotional to know what to say when we pray, He reads our unspoken feelings and knows how to help us. And He helps us according to God's will for us, which means He will help steer us away from sin if we're willing to be led.)

Getting Personal (optional):
Encouraging Students Who Struggle

Because Christian teens often suffer much needless, unspoken guilt and anger at God over how they cope with their sexual feelings, you may want at this point to discuss two sensitive, personal issues: pornography and masturbation. Adapt comments like these to reflect your or your church's stand on these issues:

Pornography, the selling of sexual images in words and pictures, is designed to grab your attention and addict you. It feeds desire, but since it will never satisfy, it can only leave you wanting more.

Pornography is a form of prostitution—models, writers, publishers, and others are directly or indirectly getting paid for providing sexual pleasure. It degrades women by portraying them as passive sex objects. And it is a complete perversion of God's purposes for sex as an expression of love and unity between two people; pornography is absolutely impersonal. A person reading or watching pornography is totally self-absorbed; in no way is he experiencing loving involvement with another person.

Outward temptations to concentrate on sex are everywhere. But the strongest source of sexual desire comes from within us, and it's essentially something good. It's our own natural drive to fulfill our physical and emotional desires and to be close to another person. These feelings are good; God gave them to us. What we do with them, as with any other good thing God gives us, may be good or bad.

Releasing sexual feelings through masturbation, for instance, is extremely common. Often it begins in early childhood, before the person even knows what masturbation is.

Bible scholars don't agree on how or whether Scripture talks about this subject. Masturbation can be highly addictive, though. It can turn inward a desire which is meant to be directed outward; it turn our sexuality, which is meant to express love and closeness with another person, into self-absorption.

But you don't have to let this problem plague you with guilt, because God offers forgiveness and healing. His desire to have a relationship with you doesn't change, even though you might struggle with your sexuality.

After completing your comments, having adapted them to fit your group and church, give kids a chance to react if they wish. Encourage those who struggle with these problems not to give up on themselves, because God hasn't. Help them to understand that, from God's perspective, their struggles with sexuality are no different from the ones they face in other areas of their lives—and that God forgives sexual sins as he forgives other kinds of wrongdoing. Point out that kids may find it helpful to talk things over later with you, your pastor, or a Christian counselor you could recommend.

No Regrets?
Refuting Arguments Against Waiting

Pass out copies of "Regretfully Yours" (Student Sheet 15). After giving kids a chance to read it, discuss possible reactions to the statements following the girl's letter. Here are some:

1. "If it's impossible to wait, how did I manage to wait for so long? It wasn't physical need that changed my mind, but pressure from the guy."

2. "I thought we were in love. That's what he kept telling me. If he really loved me, he would have waited."

3. "He said we were going to get married. After we had sex, he changed his mind."

4. "The pill isn't always effective—and it can never protect you from the hurt."

5. "If emotions aren't part of sex, why do I feel so terrible?"

After discussing answers, remind kids that God has good reasons for telling us to wait. Close in silent prayer, allowing kids to talk to God about their reactions to this session.

One of your students, a 16-year-old girl, is sitting in the back seat of a car with her boyfriend. "No," she's saying. "I might get pregnant."

"No way," the boy replies. "I've got protection."

"We might get AIDS or something," she says.

"It'll never happen to us," he counters.

"But it's wrong."

"Who says? Maybe it's wrong for your Sunday School teacher, but not for us."

The girl is wavering. "I'm just not ready."

"But I'm in love with you *now*," the guy says. "I just want to show you how special you are to me."

Saying no in a church group is easy. Saying no in the back seat of a car can be tough. Girls *and* guys need to understand the clear choices that face them, and how they can resist or flee temptation. This session is designed to help them say no when the real-life pressure's on.

Choices

The Point — To help kids see how sexual temptation gets a foothold, and to help them find ways to live by God's standards even when it's difficult.

The Passages — Genesis 39:1-12; II Timothy 2:22; James 1:13-15

The Preparation — You'll need the following:
- Bibles
- Pencils
- Copies of "Waverly Waffle and the Mysterious Package" (Student Sheet 16)
- Copies of "Creepy Crawlies" (Student Sheet 17)
- Scissors
- Large sheets or roll of paper
- Markers

Waverly Waffles
Illustrating the Process of Giving In

Step 1

Select two students to dramatize "Waverly Waffle and the Mysterious Package" (Student Sheet 16). Give copies only to those two students for now. Instead of using props, have your actors pretend to open the package, etc.

After the drama, thank your actors. Distribute copies of Student Sheet 16 to the rest of the class. Discuss:

How could Waverly have avoided his disappointment? (As soon as he received the package, he could have decided not to open it. Then he wouldn't have gone through all that agonizing.)

What caused Waverly's indecision? (He could vaguely remember some warnings about not opening a package, but he hadn't paid much attention. His curiosity was stronger than the half-remembered warnings.)

How did Sal Salivary, the delivery person, increase Waverly's desire? (Sal told Waverly that the package could be opened now and thought about later; Sal challenged and made fun of Waverly's resistance; Sal got Waverly's curiosity going.)

How does this encounter between Waverly and Sal resemble the way some people give in to premarital sex? (They remember being told they aren't supposed to, but they don't recall why; the prize looks attractive; they have a natural curiosity and they're egged on by others; people make fun of their standards; they neglect saying an early no and keep wavering between yes and no, until desire finally says yes; while they have momentary enjoyment, they later regret acting too soon and feel cheated because the prize now will never be the same; they have no one to blame but themselves.)

Where Sin Begins
Identifying Points at Which We Can Say No

Step 2

The Bible doesn't "waffle" (avoid committing itself) about the question of whether sex outside marriage is right. We hear lots of people saying it's okay if you love each other, if you're responsible, if you consider the consequences, and so forth. But the Bible doesn't rest its morality on fleeting feelings. It tells us that sexual relations are appropriate only between a man and a woman who are committed to each other in the bond of marriage.

But what are you supposed to do when you're tempted to break that rule? It's easy to say no to sex when we're sitting here, but not so easy when you actually face an opportunity to say yes. Let's try first to understand how temptation works.

Have a student read James 1:13-15. Discuss the passage along the following lines:

Where does temptation come from? (Our own evil desires—our tendency to want what's wrong. We can't blame God; we can't even say, "The devil made me do it." Adam and Eve used that excuse in the Garden of Eden, and God still held them responsible for their disobedience.) Be sure to point out that sexual feelings are not evil in themselves; the desire to act on those feelings now, no matter what God has said, is the evil part.

If you wanted to stop a sexual temptation at the "evil desire" stage, how might you do it? (Some suggestions: Understand what your desires are; ask God to help you change evil desires—such as the thrill of getting away with breaking the rules—to healthier desires; avoid things that might appeal to your desire to do wrong; concentrate on fulfilling healthy desires or on helping other people; watch out for the feeling of being enticed or dragged away instead of pretending that you're helpless.)

Sin isn't full-grown when it first appears. There are steps along the way, and we can say no at several different points. The longer we wait to say no, the tougher it gets.

Have your actors perform the "Waverly Waffle" skit again. But this time stop the action every few lines and discuss how Waverly could have resisted at that point. What could he have said or done? Was it ever too early to say no? Was it ever too late?

Joseph's Story
Learning from One Young Person Who Resisted the Pressure

Joseph had a good reaction to the offer of sex from another man's wife: He ran the other direction!

Read Genesis 39:1-12. Also look up II Timothy 2:22 and point out that Joseph was a living example of "fleeing" from lust. Ask students to imagine they are interviewing Joseph after this encounter. Discuss Joseph's possible answers to these questions:

Why didn't you take advantage of the opportunity the woman offered you?

Did you feel strongly tempted to go ahead?

How did you feel when she approached you the first time?

Why did you say no right away, instead of thinking it over?

What reasons did you have for saying no?

As she persisted, how did you handle the increased temptation?

What would you advise a young person who loves God and is being pressured to have sex?

Since these questions require students to speculate, they need not feel pressure to come up with absolutely correct answers. But they should be encouraged to think through the possibilities and try to understand Joseph's feelings and motives. Remind them that Joseph had already set a pattern of obeying God and living close to Him before this incident. Joseph was determined not to sin against God, and had already considered how God would feel if Joseph gave into this temptation (vs. 9). The solution was to run, even though it looked awkward and was later used against him. Joseph might recommend running to kids today.

The Ants Go Marching
Identifying Sources of Temptation

Distribute Student Sheet 17, "Creepy Crawlies." Give students time to work, and discuss their "ant-swers." Here are some possibilities:

Double date with couple who likes to "park": Avoid dating with this couple. If you do go out with them, arrange transportation that the other couple can't control. Try going out with a whole group so that the other couple doesn't influence you.

Your date's parents aren't home: Stay out of his or her house. Go to your house or somewhere else, preferably with friends. If necessary, don't even walk your date to his or her door. Or don't see the person until his or her parents are around.

You're lonely: Spend some time with family or friends. Visit someone who needs help. Talk to God. Help out at church. Talk to a counselor or pastor about your feelings. Avoid escaping through sexual fantasy or looking for a sexual relationship.

Your date suggests spending the night together: Say no and explain your reasons. If your date presses you, leave and call parents or friends for transportation home. Don't date the person again until he or she accepts your values.

You see porno magazines on shelf at local store: Get out of the store, and avoid it in the future if possible. If you have to shop there, avoid going alone. Read something that's interesting but not sexually oriented.

Friends invite you to video party (no adults around): Don't go. Or go with a friend who will leave with you if the videos have sexual content—and agree in advance where you will draw the line.

Your own thoughts keep turning to sexual fantasy: Turn your thoughts outward to the needs of other people. Avoid spending a lot of time alone. Find something that interests you but isn't involved with sex. Think about people as individuals God cares for, not objects to be manipulated. Figure out what tends to get the fantasies started (a TV show, self-pity, etc.) and avoid it.

Point out that often the best escape route is found in advance: not putting ourselves in the tempting situation in the first place. God promises a way out of temptation, but we shouldn't count on Him for a last-minute rescue if we've deliberately put ourselves in a tempting spot.

For example, if you deliberately park with your date in a secluded place, don't expect God to magically shut off your desires at the last second. In that case His escape route would be to use the self-control He gives long before that moment, by planning to go somewhere else more public, or deciding in advance where you'll draw the line.

Fifty Ways to Leave Your "Lover"
Practicing Responses to Tempting Situations

Have kids brainstorm creative ways to say no to a person who is trying to press them to get sexually involved. As they do so, have them write the "exit lines" on large sheets (or a roll) of paper. Suggestions may range from the serious ("I don't want to disobey God because I love Him") to the silly ("Sorry, I have to go barbecue a goldfish"). The point is to come up with as many responses as possible in the time you have.

When all the ideas are in, let each student tear a response from the paper and take it as a reminder. If you close in prayer, ask God to help kids say no in the "real" world this week.

"My youth leader and the other kids keep talking about how to stay sexually pure. And I sit there miserable because I know I've given in—more than once. Can my youth leader tell by looking at me? Do the other kids know? I feel like a hypocrite, but I'm afraid to admit that for me it's too late."

You may well have teens in your group who are, or have been, sexually involved. These sessions are for them, too. Christ died for—yes—even that sin, and kids can know His forgiveness. And He can help them keep from repeating the past.

Starting Over

The Point

To help teens see that God's forgiveness is available to those who have sinned sexually, and to help them break patterns of illicit sexual activity.

The Passages

Luke 7:36-50; John 8:3-11; Psalm 51; I John 1:8-9

The Preparation

You'll need the following:
• "Regret, Remorse, and Repentance" (Student Sheet 18)
• Bibles
• Pencils, paper

Lisa's Confession

Understanding That Sin is Sin, Sexual or Not

Step 1

Read students this story:

Lisa stopped coming to church several weeks ago. When her teacher and the other kids say they miss her, she makes excuses: "I didn't feel good last week"; "I had homework to do."

The truth is, Lisa is embarrassed to go. The subject at church lately has been honesty, and Lisa is full of guilt. She won a scholarship by cheating on several exams last year.

Lying is a habit with Lisa. She lies to her parents a lot about where she's going, and you notice she's even lying now about why she has dropped out of church. Lisa is afraid of what people will think of her. And she's afraid she won't be able to break her habit of lying.

Discuss: **If Lisa were a member of this group, and she told you the truth about herself, what could you say to help her?** (Some possibilities: That you care about her; Christ died for the sin of lying; she can confess; people will still accept her; she may even find there are other liars in the group who would also like to come clean, and they can help each other.)

Now let's alter Lisa's situation. Instead of lying, her sin is that she has had sex with several guys—not guys in the youth group. She knows it's wrong, but she's afraid of what people would think of her if she admitted what's been going on. And she doesn't know how to keep it from happening again.

What would you say to Lisa now? (Kids may have to think awhile about this. But the answers should be basically the same as for the sin of lying. The point is that when we take some sins much more seriously than others, it's harder for people who commit those "worse" sins to get help and find forgiveness.)

Friend of Sinners

Seeing Jesus' Love for People Who Have Fallen

Step 2

Divide the group into two teams. Assign one team Luke 7:36-50, and the other team John 8:3-11. Instruct the teams to find answers for these questions:

What was the sin of the person Jesus dealt with? (In the Luke passage, we don't know, though from the Pharisee's repulsion we may think she was a prostitute; in the John passage, it was clearly adultery.)

What attitude did the Pharisees have toward her? (Condemnation.)

What attitude did the Pharisees expect Christ to take toward the sinner? (In the Luke passage, the Pharisee named Simon expected Jesus to be as condemning as he was; in the John passage, they suspected He would be forgiving but would also uphold God's Law, which should put Him in a bind.)

In contrast, what attitude did Jesus have toward the sinner? (Forgiveness and the desire for her to lead a new life.)

Did Jesus belittle the person's sin? (No; He took the sin seriously and treated it as real, but He also forgave the sinner.)

What were His final words to the sinner? (He assured her of His forgiveness and assumed she would lead a new and different life in harmony with God's will.)

Forgiveness Update
Being Assured That Christ Still Forgives Sexual Sin

Talk about where you think your group might be in terms of guilt over sexual activity. If you like, adapt the following:

It's hard for a lot of adults to imagine the sexual pressures you face today. It's hard for us to know how different and lonely you may feel if you're trying to obey God.

Some in this group may have already yielded to the pressure. Maybe you've had sex once or twice and you still feel guilty. You're too ashamed to believe that God can forgive you. Perhaps some of you are in a sexual relationship and can't—or won't—find the strength to end it. Chances are that many of you have problems with sexual thoughts and actions that just won't seem to go away.

A lot of adults have also sat in church feeling guilty about some sin, hoping nobody knew. Christ died for those sins, and yours, and He stands ready to forgive, as He forgave the people in the Scripture passages we just read.

That doesn't mean that God just excuses or overlooks sin. He took our sin seriously enough to require the death of His own Son to pay for it. He asks for repentance as well as faith. Repentance means changing our minds and turning away from sin.

Distribute Student Sheet 18, "Regret, Remorse, and Repentance." Have kids take turns reading Psalm 51 aloud. Then give them time to complete the sheet individually and share the results. The prayers they write will vary, of course. Some might resemble these samples:

Regret—"I wish I hadn't committed adultery. Now everyone knows what I did. If only I'd been somewhere else that night I first saw Bathsheba. I feel so guilty and depressed. At least I could have been more careful about it, so that nobody would find out. Oh, if only I'd obeyed You, Lord."

Remorse—"Oh, what a terrible thing I did. Two terrible things: committing adultery with Bathsheba and having her husband killed. It's all my fault that our baby died. I'm a rotten person, an adulterer and a murderer and a liar. Nothing will ever be the same. I'm sure You could never forgive me."

Repentance—"Wash away all my iniquity and cleanse me from my sin. For I know my transgressions. . . . Create in me a pure heart, O God. . . and grant me a willing spirit to sustain me. . . .O Lord, open my lips, and my mouth will declare your praise."

Emphasize the hope as well as brokenness that repentance includes. Encourage kids to think about which of these "three R's" they've been applying to their guilt.

Second Chances
Confessing and Moving On

Suppose "Lisa"—the second one, the one whose sin is sexual—comes back to Christ and back to church. She's confessed her sin and wants her life to be clean. But she's still an attractive girl who wants an active social life. What plan can Lisa make to keep from getting sexually involved again?

(Some possibilities: dating Christians who share her moral standards; she and her boyfriend can decide in advance, together, that sex is not going to happen; dates can be planned to steer away from places, situations, and company where sex is strongly encouraged; if pressured, she can say no early instead of walking the fence; she should enlist the support of sympathetic friends, church youth workers, and—yes—even her parents to help her stay faithful to the standards Christ has given her.)

Read I John 1:8-9 and suggest that students memorize it. **God offers His forgiveness in Christ no matter what we have done; He asks that we honestly and humbly admit our sin and our need for His forgiveness, and that we turn from our sin. That's as true of sexual sin as it is of any other, and that's something to thank Him for.**

If you wish, close with silent prayers of confession and thanks.

Your Order, Please

In each of the following lists, number the items to show the order of importance they have to you. Put a 1 by the most important, 2 by the second most important, etc.

LIST A
____ Getting my picture in the school news-paper
____ Regularly dating a good-looking person
____ Getting straight A's
____ Collecting all the albums of my favorite recording artist

LIST B
____ Going to college
____ Winning $10,000 in a sweepstakes
____ Getting my driver's license
____ Being a virgin

LIST C
____ Being elected to student government
____ Having others think of me as sexy
____ Learning to speak another language
____ Being good at telling jokes

LIST D
____ Getting a good job after I graduate
____ Getting married
____ Having children
____ Being famous

LIST E
____ Having others think of me as a good listener
____ Having others think of me as being sexually experienced
____ Having others think of me as fun to be around
____ Having others think of me as being a Christian

LIST F
____ Seeing my favorite group in concert
____ Reading an exciting novel
____ Watching an X-rated video
____ Going skiing

LIST G
____ Feeling forgiven for my sins
____ Feeling confident in front of a group
____ Feeling like I'm going to "score" on a date
____ Feeling like the smartest person in the school

LIST H
____ Being a good athlete
____ Having a sexual relationship before marriage
____ Appearing on a TV game show
____ Knowing a lot about the Bible

A Sure Way for Scorched Feet

Read Proverbs 6:20, 27-29 and Hebrews 13:4. In Proverbs, what are the results of adultery compared to?

This guy is about to take a stroll onto the "hot coals" of sexual immorality. But he's going to get burned. On each "coal" write one possible result of going against God's perspective on sex. (The results could be immediate or long-term.)

Friends Unafraid

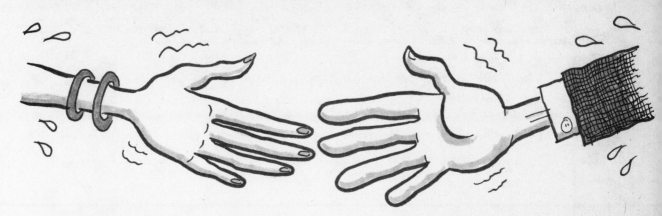

Have you ever hesitated to be "just friends" with someone of the opposite sex because of what people might think? Jesus, Paul, and others in the Bible formed close friendships with people of the opposite sex. These spiritual leaders knew their enemies were eager to find fault with them, but they risked criticism and misunderstanding anyway. For example:

Read Luke 8:1-3. Who traveled with Jesus? How many were men? How many were women?

What rumors might Jesus' enemies have spread about Him and His companions?

Note: At that time and in that culture, women were not looked upon as men's equals. Jesus dared to break some molds in His relationships!

Read John 11:1-5. Jesus was not married, and apparently neither were Lazarus, Mary, or Martha. Other Scriptures tell us He had stayed in their home. What does this Scripture tell you about the kind of friendships Jesus formed?

Read Acts 16:13-15. "We" apparently refers to Luke, the writer of Acts, as well as to Paul. When the missionaries discovered only women at the place of prayer, what might they have done to fit in with the custom of the day?

What did they do instead?

With what results?

The Buddy System

Check off the answers that best apply to you. (Don't worry, it's private!)

I realize that I've been looking on members of the opposite sex as:

___ a way to not be bored on Friday and Saturday nights

___ status symbols (if they'll go out with me)

___ people I don't understand

___ people who'll hurt you if you let them

___ people God loves as much as He loves me

___ (other): _____

To improve my friendships with the opposite sex, I'm going to:

___ start having real conversations with some of them

___ stop picking on them

___ call up one of them just to talk

___ listen when one of them talks

___ (other): _____

If somebody misinterprets my friendship with the opposite sex,
I'm going to:

___ break off my friendship

___ smile and say, "We're just friends."

___ quote all of today's lesson from memory

___ smile and say, "We're just friends; why don't you mind your own business, you nosy jerk?"

___ constantly wonder what everybody's thinking about me

___ (other): _____

Worth Waiting For?

What's the maximum length of time you would wait for the following things?

a hot dog _____

a date who's late _____

in line for the latest movie _____

in line for a movie you've seen before _____

a phone call about a job _____

the right person to marry _____

a salesperson to notice you in a clothing store _____

your Sunday School teacher or youth leader who's late _____

a touring rock star whose concert doesn't start on time _____

finding the right car to buy _____

a chance to be in the Olympics _____

your friend to come to know Christ _____

Regretfully Yours

The following letter is real. It was written by a teenage girl, who sent it to youth leader Joe White (who quoted it in his book Friendship Pressure, *published by Operation Challenge, Branson, Missouri).*

"Since I started dating I have always promised myself that I would stay a virgin until I was married. I have lived [up] to that promise until the past year. [My boyfriend] said that he loved me and like all of the others, we would get married. I really believed that he loved me.

After our first time, I started taking the pill to keep from getting pregnant. Two months later he dropped me for his old girlfriend (who was once pregnant by him). I felt as if I had 200 knives go through me. I was crushed."

Pretending for a moment that you wrote this letter, read the following statements by people who think it's stupid to wait until marriage to have sex. How do you respond to them, based on the experience described in your letter?

1. "It's physically impossible to wait."

2. "You don't have to be married to have sex, as long as you're in love."

3. "It's OK if you're planning to get married eventually."

4. "It's OK as long as you use 'protection.'"

5. "Sex is just a physical thing. There's no need to make a big emotional deal out of it."

Waverly Waffle
And the Mysterious Package

Characters:

> WAVERLY WAFFLE (hereafter known as **W.W.**), a normal person
> SAL SALIVARY   (**S.S.** from now on), a delivery person for Untied Parcel

There is a knock at the door. W.W. opens it, to find S.S. on the doorstep, holding a wrapped package.

W.W.: Yes? What do you want?

> **S.S.:** Untied Parcel. Package for W. Waffle.

W.W.: Huh? For me?

> **S.S.:** That's what it says, isn't it? Sign here.

W.W.: (Takes the package, signs, then hesitates) Wait a minute. I think I'm not supposed to have this yet.

> **S.S.:** Huh? But it's yours.

W.W. (thinking): Yes, but—I remember something about not opening a package that was coming for me because—oh, rats, I can't remember.

> **S.S.:** Well, why don't you open it now? You can remember later.

W.W.: Well, I really don't think I should. . .

> **S.S.:** Come on, aren't you curious about what it is? (peering at W.W.) Who told you you weren't supposed to have this yet?

W.W.: My parents, I think. Or maybe it was my Sunday School teacher. Or my church. I forget.

> **S.S.:** Well, you know what they're like. If you wait for their permission to get anything, you'll be 110.

W.W.: I don't think that was why—there was some other reason . . .

> **S.S.:** Look, I haven't got all day. The suspense is killing me.

W.W.: (starts to open package; hesitates again) Well, I don't know if I should . . .

> **S.S.:** "Should?" What's with all these "shoulds?" Who says what you should or shouldn't do?

W.W.: I do! But there was some reason why it wasn't good for me to . . . oh, I'll go ahead. No, I won't. Yes, I will. No, I won't.

> **S.S.:** Make up your mind. What's your answer?

W.W.: It's no. I guess. I think.

> **S.S.:** Are you sure?

W.W.: Sort of.

> **S.S.:** (shrugs) Okay, your loss. (starts to walk away)

W.W.: Wait a minute! I changed my mind! (grabs package, starts to rip it open. As he opens it, W.W. continues talking to self) After all, it's mine, isn't it? It isn't good mental health to frustrate myself. I was going to get this eventually anyway, so what difference does it make when? Studies have shown that . . . (package is now open; S.S. stares) It's that computer I wanted! But what's in this card? (opens card, reads) "Happy Birthday, Waverly, from Aunt Jenny and Uncle Russ." But my birthday's not for months! Oh, no, I opened my birthday present early! Now I won't look forward to it!

> **S.S.:** But you can enjoy it, right? Oops, looks like it got a little damaged when you grabbed it. Well, I don't care, I just deliver the goods. 'Bye. (S.S. exits, leaving W.W. holding the bag . . . or package.)

CURTAIN

Creepy Crawlies

"So, if you think you are standing firm, be careful that you don't fall! No temptation has seized you except what is common to man. And God is faithful; he will not let you be tempted beyond what you can bear. But when you are tempted, he will also provide a way out so that you can stand up under it" (I Corinthians 10:12-13).

Help! You're a prisoner in an ant farm! Each of these "ants" stands for a possible source of sexual temptation. What might be a God-given escape route from each one? Write a word or two describing your escape plan in each tunnel.

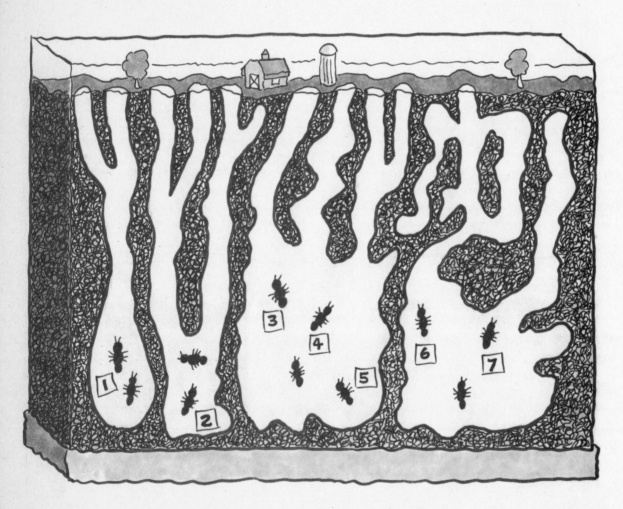

1. A double date with couple who likes to "park"

2. Your date's parents aren't home

3. You see porno magazines on shelf at local store

4. Your own thoughts keep turning to sexual fantasy

5. You're lonely

6. Your date suggests spending the night together

7. Friends invite you to video party (no adults around)

If you think these "ants" are too easy to escape, label the "blank ants" with some temptations you think are really tough!

Regret, Remorse, and Repentance

King David committed adultery, and God let him know that He knew. The Lord brought David around to repentance, and God forgave him. Psalm 51 is the prayer David wrote after that experience.

Write a short prayer David might have written if he felt only REGRET (wishing he hadn't done what he did):

Write a short prayer he might have written if he felt only REMORSE (feeling hopelessly sorry for himself):

Now find phrases from Psalm 51 which show David's true REPENTANCE (honestly acknowledging his sin and turning away from it toward God):

How to Talk to Kids About Doubts

by James Long

I met Janice on a Sunday night not long ago. My friend Chris and I found ourselves sitting next to her on an airplane. There Chris and I were, second to the last row, with a jet engine roaring in one ear and young, beer-guzzling, depressed Janice murmuring in the other.

I was glad I had a rough idea of what to say to someone deep in doubt, for it wasn't long before Janice, religious from birth, voiced her struggle to believe. She marveled, open-mouthed, that Chris and I might admit to unanswerable questions, yet hold to faith in a Christ who lives and cares. Hard experiences had left Janice jaded and doubtful.

We dive into this unit of sessions with Janice and her frail faith in mind. We look at doubt, knowing we confront it often—when believers feel free enough to say they don't always believe. We dig into Scripture for perspective on hardship, realizing, in our honest moments, that we have questions, too.

Nine Suggestions

How do you talk to kids about doubts, then? Here are a few thoughts that have been helpful to me.

1. When kids express doubt, don't panic. Generally, a doubter's questions make us nervous because we feel we can't adequately answer them, or because we sense the person doesn't really want answers, or because it seems irreverent to question God or the Bible.

Relax. God can handle our questions, and the success of this person's faith does not rest solely (or even principally) with you.

2. When kids express doubt, listen! Job is not the only person who has been deeply hurt by people who spoke when they should have listened. Hurting people often—in my experience, almost always—complain of "helpers" who would not listen. Proverbs puts it this way: "Even a fool is thought wise if he keeps silent, and discerning if he holds his tongue" (17:28). Many grief- and hardship-related struggles are gradually resolved through simply talking and listening. They talk. You listen.

3. When kids express doubt, don't argue. All

judgment has been entrusted to the Son (John 5:22). There is a reason for that: We are not qualified to judge. At times of extreme doubt, people often express strong feelings, even considerably overstating their objections. They may be sharply critical of God, the pastor, their parents, you, everyone. Put aside defensiveness.

4. When kids express doubt, help them identify its source. James reminds us that "He who doubts is like a wave of the sea, blown and tossed by the wind" (1:6). But there are different breeds of doubt. Some is triggered by hardship and suffering, some when a person we love dies or is disabled by disease. We may wonder about war or hunger. Dad may be out of work; friends may betray us; we may feel ugly. In the face of all kinds of pain, we may wonder about God.

Don't rush ahead with premature answers. Listen, then gradually point toward the help and perspective found in Scripture and worked out in your experience.

Doubts may also rise from legitimate intellectual questions. The Bible seems to contradict itself; we can't square creation and evolution; we wonder about the Virgin Birth.

Answer honest intellectual questions if you are prepared to do so, or suggest books that seek to reconcile faith and reason. Don't be afraid to admit your own ignorance. "I don't know" is sometimes an admirable answer. And don't allow yourself to be pulled into arguing (II Timothy 2:23, 24). That's unproductive.

Sometimes doubters are like the man who told Jesus, "I do believe; help me overcome my unbelief!" (Mark 9:24). Other times, doubt bubbles up out of an inner core of unbelief; the message is never combined with faith (Hebrews 4:2). Sometimes a caring word of warning is appropriate. But consider Galatians 6:1 first: "If a man is trapped in some sin, you who are spiritual should restore him gently. But watch yourself, or you also may be tempted."

The challenge we place before doubters: Will we bring our pain and questions to a God who hurts with us, even if we must wait for satisfying answers? Will we face our intellectual questions honestly, willing to study and read open-mindedly? Will we bring our disbelief under the scrutiny of Scripture (Hebrews 4:11-13)?

5. When kids express doubt, ask key questions. Rather than sermonizing, provoke thought. "Have you thought of it this way?" "What makes you feel that way?" "Is it possible you are angry at God about . . .?"

6. When kids express doubt, use Scripture wisely. We may be capable of clever expression, but Scripture has the power (John 17:17). Don't quote it glibly, but do quote it.

7. When kids express doubt, remind them that they are in good company. Job was labeled "blameless and upright" (1:8), yet in the heat of trial his faith seemed to wilt. He complained that God seemed to ignore him and even to tear him down (Job 19:6-11). Jeremiah vented similar feelings (Lamentations 3:7-9). Even Jesus fell into unfathomable emotional distress in Gethsemane as He wrestled with the unfolding of the Father's will (Mark 14:33-36). From the cross he expressed His desperate aloneness: "My God, my God, why have you forsaken me?" (Mark 15:34).

Job, Jeremiah, and Jesus also made great pronouncements of faith, of course. "I know that my Redeemer lives" (Job 19:25); "Great is your faithfulness" (Lamentations 3:23); "Not what I will, but what you will" (Mark 14:36). But still, there were the questions, the doubts.

When kids come to us with doubts, we must help them put their questions in perspective: People of great faith have struggled with doubt. God understands our sense of panic in the face of overwhelming hardship or questions that we cannot quell.

8. When kids express doubt, remind them that their faith is still under construction. Often doubt is merely faith struggling for firm footing, trying to make belief and life agree. True, "We live by faith, not by sight" (II Corinthians 5:7); and "Blessed are those who have not seen and yet have believed" (John 20:29). Yet we must sometimes work to reconcile faith and experience. At times that work will look and feel like doubt.

9. When kids express doubt, help them nurture a "forever perspective." I know of nothing more effective in fighting doubts than this: View today through the window of forever.

Skim II Corinthians 11:23-29. It enumerates Paul's struggles. You may wonder, *How could this guy go on? Why wasn't he paralyzed by doubts?* The answer: He had perspective.

"We do not lose heart. Though outwardly we are wasting away, yet inwardly we are being renewed day by day. For our light and momentary troubles are achieving for us an eternal glory that far outweighs them all. So we fix our eyes not on what is seen, but on what is unseen. For what is seen is temporary, but what is unseen is eternal" (II Corinthians 4:16-18).

To cope, kids must be able to look beyond today. Or, more accurately, they must be able to look at today through the window of forever. Today's troubles, however distressing, are light and momentary. But they only appear that way in contrast to an eternal glory.

Hebrews 11 reminds all of us sometimes-doubters that there are rewards for honest seekers. And they come through faith.

Taking the Risk

What happened to Janice, the young woman on our flight who had such struggles and questions? I wish I could say that I finished our conversation with the certainty that she had turned back, in faith, to the One she doubted. I can't. Instead I have a pitiful picture in my mind of a desperate girl, deep in thought, standing by a baggage carousel at the airport, waiting for her luggage and feeling terribly alone.

My comfort is this: When God put me in the back of that 727, I was, thanks to His grace, prepared to listen and respond when someone needed to voice her doubts.

Because of that, I write this with a heightened sense of your importance—you who listen as kids take the risk of sharing their doubts.

Jim Long is senior editor of Campus Life *magazine. The author of several books, including* How Could God Let This Happen? *(Tyndale), he has been involved in street evangelism and youth work at the church and denominational levels.*

Doubts

by John Duckworth

John Duckworth is the author of four books including *The School Zone* (Victor) and *Joan 'n' the Whale and Other Stories You Never Heard in Sunday School* (Revell). He's taught young people in Sunday Schools and youth groups, and spends most of his waking hours as Senior Editor of Church Resources for the David C. Cook Publishing Co. He admits to having doubted on numerous occasions.

It happened in biology class, when Jeannie saw that "Tree of Life" evolutionary diagram for the first time. It happened when Terry prayed that his parents would get back together, and they got a divorce. It happened when Nguyen was rejected by racist kids in a "Christian" school.

It's doubt. Surely every Christian has known it, teenagers foremost among them. There is plenty to doubt about Christianity, and plenty of reasons to doubt it. There are the obvious ones: the skepticism of a school teacher, the fall of a TV preacher, or the refusal of a relative or romantic interest to accept Christ. But there are also the more subtle, everyday ones: a misunderstood Bible verse, a feeling that non-Christians have more fun, or the simple inability to see the spiritual realm.

To be human is to doubt. There is no way to protect kids from it, and that's a good thing. Kids need to question before they can truly believe. Unfortunately, for too many young people doubt leads to guilt, suppression, and even rejection of the faith. Kids need answers, but they also need to learn how to live with doubt.

That's why this sesson begins at the beginning. It addresses a question that may be keeping some of your students from dealing with their doubts: "Is God mad at me for doubting Him?"

Look Out for
Lightning!

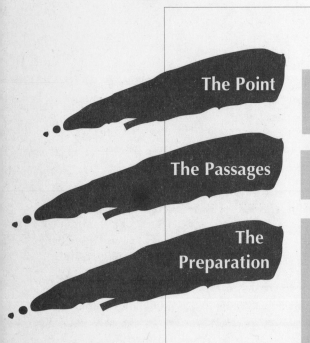

The Point	To help kids understand that it's all right to have doubts about their faith, and that God wants to help them resolve doubts.
The Passages	Matthew 11:1-11; Mark 9:24; Luke 24:36-45; Psalm 34:4-8; Jude 22
The Preparation	You'll need the following: • A supermarket tabloid newspaper • Copies of "Sign on the Doubted Line" (Student Sheet 19) • Anti-perspirant (one can or roll-on stick) • Pencils • Bibles • Copies of "Shocking Secrets" (Student Sheet 20)

Inquiring Minds Want to Know
Discovering the Good and Bad Sides of Doubt

Bring to class one or two copies of a sensationalistic tabloid newspaper (the kind sold at supermarket checkout counters) which you've cut into single pages. (Be sure to scan the photos and articles beforehand to screen out material you feel is inappropriate.) Articles will probably feature headlines like, "Ghost of Elvis Haunts Siamese Twins," "Bigfoot Sees UFO Crash in Bermuda Triangle," and "Psychic Predicts President to Lose 100 Pounds on Amazing Mouthwash Diet."

Distribute pages to the group and let kids spend a couple of minutes laughing at the stories. Then ask: **Which of these articles do you believe? Which do you find hard to believe? Why?**

As you discuss kids' reactions, point out that we tend to believe ideas that (1) match our own experiences, (2) agree with what we've been told by people we trust, or (3) have been verified by several sources. Many of the tabloid tales don't fit those guidelines.

Ask: **How might your life be different if you believed everything you heard or read?** (You'd never think for yourself; you'd be so mixed up you couldn't accomplish anything; people could easily take advantage of you; you'd have to believe contradictory statements; you'd be superstitious, nervous, etc.)

Ask how doubt could actually help a person in the following situations:

1. You approach a rickety-looking bridge and doubt whether it would hold you up. (Doubt could cause you to take another route and avoid injury.)

2. You doubt the word of a car salesman who says a 10-year-old car has only 5,000 miles on it. (Doubt could keep you from being cheated.)

3. You doubt a friend who says that taking cocaine won't hurt you. (You'd say no and avoid getting addicted.)

So being able to doubt is sometimes a good thing. It can keep us and others from getting hurt. But how can doubt hurt us? (Too much of it can make us afraid to take risks or trust anybody.)

What about doubting God, the Bible, the church, or anything else that has to do with being a Christian? Does that help or hurt? (Opinions will probably vary, depending on the type of doubt. Challenge kids who say doubts are all bad or all good, but don't try to reach consensus. The more disagreement there is at this point, the better.)

Before we try to figure out an answer to that question, let's find out whether doubts about Christianity affect us, or just "other" people.

Never Let Them See You Sweat
Admitting Doubts About Our Faith

Distribute copies of Student Sheet 19, "Sign on the Doubted Line." Explain that this game is a sort of scavenger hunt. When you give the signal, kids are to get up and try to find others in the group who fit the numbered descriptions on the sheet. The object is to get each blank initialed by one person who fits the description, with no person signing more than one blank. (If there are fewer than 10 in your group, allow kids to sign two blanks each.) The first person to get all the blanks initialed wins. If no one gets all blanks signed in two minutes, stop the game and declare the person with the most signed blanks to be the winner.

Award a can or stick of anti-perspirant to the winner (in case of a tie, tell them they'll have to share.) Explain: **You may be wondering why the prize is an anti-perspirant. It's not because the winner smells! It's because there used to be an anti-perspirant commercial on TV that said, "Never let them see you sweat." The idea was to keep people from knowing when you were nervous.**

We're the same way about our doubts sometimes. Why might we be afraid to let other people know our doubts about God? (They might look down on us, get mad, or doubt God, too.) **Why might we be afraid to let God know about our doubts?** (He might not like our lack of faith.) **Sometimes we're even afraid to admit doubts to ourselves. Why?** (Maybe we're afraid that if we doubt one thing, our whole faith will fall apart.)

As time and the openness of your group allow, discuss the doubts kids initialed on "Sign on the Doubted Line." How do doubts make your students feel? Encourage them to look for God's view of doubt as you move on to the next activity.

Distinguished Doubters
Exploring God's Responses To People's Doubts

Step 3

Divide the group into four teams. Assign each team to look at the following passages:

Team A: Matthew 11:1-11
Team B: Mark 9:20-27
Team C: Luke 24:36-45; Psalm 34:4-8; Jude 22
Team D: Matthew 8:23-27

Each team should be prepared to answer the following question about its verses: **What can we learn from this passage about the way the Lord reacts to people's doubts?**

After allowing kids to examine their verses for a few minutes, have each team report. Use the following information to supplement their findings as needed.

Team A: John the Baptist was in prison (Matthew 11:1-11). He wasn't sure whether Jesus was really the Messiah, so he sent his followers to question Jesus. Jesus told the messengers to tell John about the miracles they saw Jesus perform. Instead of criticizing John for doubting, Jesus offered His actions as evidence. Then Jesus told the crowds that John was one of the greatest people ever born. Jesus' opinion of John was still very high despite John's questioning. That seems to indicate that the Lord isn't offended by honest questions, and that some of the things He's done are meant as evidence to help people believe.

Team B: A man brought his demon-possessed son to Jesus (Mark 9:20-27), wanting Jesus to heal the boy "if He could." Jesus said, "All things are possible to him who believes." Jesus wasn't making a blanket promise to "perform" for anyone who believed, but was saying that the man's faith wasn't very strong. The man said, "I believe; help my unbelief!" Jesus' response was to heal the boy. The Lord didn't demand that the man become 100% doubt-free. The man believed as much as he could at that point, and asked Jesus to help with his doubts. It's good to know that God understands that we're a mixture of faith and doubt. He responds to our honest requests for help with our doubts.

Team C: In Luke 24:36-45, Jesus appeared to his followers after He rose from the dead. They weren't sure whether He was real. Instead of giving them an angry lecture on God's power, Jesus invited them to look at His wounds, touch Him, and watch Him eat a piece of fish—all to show that He was real. In Psalm 34:4-8, David writes about how God answered His fears—and invites people to "taste and see that the Lord is good." In Jude 22 we're advised to "convince some, who doubt." Taking all these verses together, we get the idea that God is patient with honest doubts, and that He sometimes appeals to our physical senses and our minds to help us believe.

Team D: Having spent some time with Jesus and seen some of His miracles, the disciples should have known that Jesus had amazing power. But when a storm came up (Matthew 8:23-27), they panicked. Jesus asked, "Why are you afraid, O men of little faith?" Then he calmed the storm.

Why did Jesus criticize the disciples for their doubts? Maybe because He'd already done so much to strengthen their faith. We need to keep this in mind, especially if we've been Christians for a while. Our doubts may not disappear, but we can learn from our experiences with God. That's better than "tasting" forever and never growing in our faith. But if we remind ourselves and each other of what He's done in the past, it gets easier to believe for the future.

Wrap up your discussion of these passages by asking volunteers to tell which of the following they most identify with today as believers or doubters: John the Baptist; the man whose son needed healing; the disciples in the boat; or David, who had just seen God answer some of his questions. Let kids who are willing explain why they feel that way. Share your own answer, too.

Shocking Secrets
Remembering that Our Doubts Aren't Shocking to God

Pass out copies of "Shocking Secrets" (Student Sheet 20). Have two or three students take turns reading the article aloud.

When the reading is done, ask: **Why was the writer of the article shocked by his friends' doubts?** (He wasn't used to discussing doubts; he was used to giving "right" answers; he had buried his own doubts; he thought his friends were such strong Christians they couldn't doubt; he thought doubters were hypocrites.)

Do you think we're faking Christianity when we doubt? (Answers may vary. Point out that we don't have to fake our faith; like the man in Mark 9, we can have some belief, some doubt, and make progress when we're honest enough to ask God for help.)

Do you think God is shocked by our doubts? (No, since He knows everything.) **Do you think God cares about our doubts?** (Yes, judging from the examples studied today—but be sensitive to kids who are doubting God's care in general.)

If you have time, let kids know about a doubt you had when you were a teenager. Perhaps it was a question about science and the Bible, or the feeling that God didn't care about a problem you had. Don't try to give the impression that all your struggles are resolved now; just admit that you've doubted, too.

Wind up the session by asking kids to think of the most "shocking" doubt they have about being Christians. Allow a couple of minutes for silent prayer, during which students can tell God about that doubt and ask Him to help. Close by thanking God for understanding our doubts and being patient with us. If you can, offer to help kids find answers to specific questions they may have in upcoming weeks.

If you could ask God 1 question about something that bothers you, what would it be?

What 1 thing about life do you wish God would change?

Are Christians crazy? They believe in an invisible, seemingly silent God. They claim to talk to a Man who was executed nearly 2,000 years ago. They try to pattern their lives after an ancient book which is ignored or ridiculed by many of the world's most respected scholars.

No wonder many teenagers feel, with Mark Twain, that faith is "believing something you know ain't so." Worse yet, some Christians build a wall between faith and reason, as if thinking were strictly the devil's territory. The fact is that faith and reason can work together in the search for truth.

This session is designed to assure kids that Christianity is not unreasonable. Your students will be led to see that even though believing may be hard, it isn't brainless. You won't answer all your kids' questions, but you may take the edge off their next bout with doubt.

(Note: This session looks at the "big picture" of faith and reason. For discussions of specific issues such as the Bible's reliability or the problem of evil, see other units in the *Hot Topics Youth Electives* series, including "Tough Questions.")

Too Hard to Believe

The Point	To help students discuss the frustrations of believing what they can't see, and to help them discover that reason plays a role in healthy faith.
The Passages	Hebrews 11; Romans 1:18-20; Genesis 1:27; II Timothy 3:16; John 14:8, 9; 20:24-31
The Preparation	You'll need the following: • Two blindfolds • Chalkboard and chalk or newsprint and markers • Copies of "Get This Straight" (Student Sheet 21) • Pencils • Bibles • Copy of "Dueling Believers" (Student Sheet 22) cut up and given to role players before class

Blind Faith
Feeling the Frustration of Acting Without Seeing

Bring two blindfolds—scarves will do if they're heavy enough—to class. Blindfold two volunteers, and put each in front of a chalkboard or large sheet of newsprint. Give each one chalk or a marker, plus a whispered assignment to draw a person or object of your choosing. Don't let the group know what the assignment is.

Allow your artists one minute to complete their masterpieces. Then see whether the other kids can guess what the drawings portray. Successful guessers could be blindfolded and given a shot at sightless drawing, too.

When the artistry's done, ask participants how it felt to draw without seeing. What was most frustrating about it?

Observe that living as a Christian sometimes feels the same way. **How many of you have ever seen God? How many have seen Jesus—not paintings, but the actual Person? How about an angel? How many have seen the earth created, or the Red Sea parted, or anyone brought back from the dead?** (You probably won't get any serious takers. If kids start to argue about modern miracles they've heard of, keep the discussion short to avoid getting side-tracked.)

Many of the most important things and persons Christians believe in are invisible to us. Do you ever wish you could take off the "blindfold" that keeps us from seeing what we believe? How might things be different if you could?

Allow kids to speculate and to express their frustrations over not being able to see God, Bible events, the return of Christ, etc. Ask how things might be different if we could hear God's voice as clearly as some Bible characters did.

If somebody said to you, "You don't need to see or hear anything; just have faith," how would you feel? What would you say—or want to say? (Kids will probably be dissatisfied with such a pat answer.) **Answers like that don't seem to help when we're frustrated. We may end up doubting that Christianity makes any sense at all. So we're going to look for some better answers today.**

Faith Value
Discovering What Faith Is

Pass out Bibles, pencils, and copies of "Get This Straight" (Student Sheet 21). Working in groups, kids should look up the verses and correct the statements about faith. When they're done, have them share their findings. As needed, add the following observations.

1. Faith is being sure of things we hope for—things we can't see at the moment. Faith is what makes up for our inability to see things that (a) aren't physical, (b) haven't happened yet, or (c) happened in the past. Faith is not just wishing something would be true, or pretending it's true when it isn't.

2. It takes faith for anybody to believe God created the universe. After all, none of us were around at the time.

3. God doesn't promise to show off in order to "prove" that He's there. If we seriously and honestly seek Him, He'll eventually reward us. A serious seeker has to exercise a little faith to at least believe God is there, somewhere.

4. Some of the "superstars" of Hebrews 11 saw some of God's promises fulfilled in their lifetimes (Abraham saw Isaac born, Noah saw the flood, etc.) But God's promise to send a Messiah didn't come true until Jesus came to

earth, long after these people had died.

5. At times God has promised something and delivered it right away—as He did at the Red Sea and Jericho. Even then people had to exercise faith, though; the Israelites had to follow Moses to the sea and march around the walls with Joshua.

6. Rahab was a prostitute, but God saved her life because of her faith.

7. Faith has enabled some to survive danger, govern countries, and win battles.

8. Being faithful has caused some to be persecuted, homeless, poor, tortured, or killed. Their hope was for what would happen *after* those things.

9. The people in Hebrews 11 were full of faith, which pleased God. Yet they didn't "receive what had been promised" (they didn't see the Messiah).

Based on the experiences of people in this chapter, do you think faith in God is easy or hard? Why? (Let kids express opinions. Point out that faith seems hard most of the time, except when we see the results. And sometimes the results aren't what we'd choose.)

If faith is so tough, why bother? Maybe there's a better, easier way to live—without faith. Let's see where that road leads.

Dueling Believers
Discovering that Every Philosophy Requires Faith

Before class, cut a copy of "Dueling Believers" (Student Sheet 22) into parts as indicated on the sheet. Assign characters to six students (double up if you don't have enough kids), allowing them time before class to read their monologues and understand their characters. When you reach this step in the session, introduce the characters one at a time and have them read their parts. Discuss each reading with the whole group, using the following questions:

What unseen thing or person does this character believe in?
How reliable is the object of this person's faith?
Suggested answers:

1. Starla Wonder believes that unseen forces caused by the movements of the planets influence what happens to her. She is putting her trust in astrologers, whose horoscopes are often so vague that they're meaningless.

2. Kerry Reasoner believes in the power of his mind to figure everything out. He thinks he uses reason *instead* of faith, but his faith is *in* reason. He trusts only his mind, but the mind can make mistakes.

3. Kurt McKult believes that his guru knows the truth. His faith is in Shreelee Rajwheelie. But the guru is a human being whose teachings are no more reliable than anyone else's, logically speaking.

4. Charlotte Darwin believes in nothing that can't be shown scientifically. Her faith is in a principle: that everything worth knowing can be proved by science. Trouble is, that principle itself can't be proved scientifically. Neither can a theory about the beginnings of life, since the beginning was a historical event; it can't be repeated in a laboratory.

5. Parr D. Animal lives by his physical senses—to feel good. He believes that there is nothing more important to life. In a way he's like Kerry Reasoner; if he can't perceive it with his brain, it's not real. His faith is in the power of his mind and body to sense everything important. But the senses, like the mind, can make mistakes.

6. Liv N. Letliv believes in a god of her own design. Unlike the One in the Bible, this god hasn't let us know what truth is. So everyone's guess is as good as everyone else's. Her god is only as reliable as she is, since she made him up.

Even if we dump Christianity, we're stuck with some kind of faith. Everybody believes in something. So the question is: Does it make sense to place our faith in the God of the Bible instead of somewhere else?

Not-So-Blind Faith
Affirming the Reasonableness of Biblical Faith

Step 4

Blindfold a volunteer who drew a picture during the first part of the session. His or her assignment is to draw the same thing as before—but with help. Guide the artist with verbal directions ("Start higher on the page," "Make a three-inch line and stop," etc.) to ensure that the drawing is as accurate as possible.

After a minute or two of drawing, compare the results with those from the earlier exercise. The second picture may not be totally accurate, but will probably outshine the first.

Ask the artist: **Why was it easier to draw this time?** (Directions were given by someone who could see.) **Did you trust my directions?** (Answers will vary, but most will have some appreciation for the help.) **If you and I had done this successfully before, how would it affect your level of trust?** (Trust would be greater.)

After thanking participants, point out that God, like the artist's helper, hasn't left us completely "in the dark" where faith is concerned. Even though He is invisible, He has given us some visible evidence that can strengthen our faith. Choose kids to read the following verses aloud and name the evidence suggested in each.

1. *Romans 1:18-20.* God has made His existence and His qualities plain in the way He made the universe.

2. *Genesis 1:27.* Since we are made in God's image, some of our traits (creativity, leadership, an eternal soul, etc.) reflect the way He is.

3. *II Timothy 3:16.* God inspired the descriptions of Him that are recorded in the Bible.

4. *John 14:8, 9.* Jesus came to earth as God in the flesh—the best picture we have of what God the Father is like.

God doesn't say, "Have faith," and leave it at that. He appeals to our senses and our reason as well. Not all this evidence is in the Bible or creation, either. Has anything ever happened to you or someone you know that strengthened your belief that God is there? (Given time, kids may think of answered prayers, provision, or other experiences. Be ready with an example from your own life, too.)

The longer we have an active relationship with God and see Him doing things in our lives, the more we tend to trust Him. It's like our blindfolded artists. If they practiced a few times with their helpers, their trust in those helpers would increase. Pretty soon they might actually produce some decent drawings!

Even so, Christianity can be hard to believe. Our doubts aren't all that surprising. Maybe that's why Jesus said what He did in the famous "Doubting Thomas" episode.

Read John 20:24-29, with emphasis on verse 29. **It's as if Jesus is sending us a message: "I know it's going to be harder for you to believe in Me. But it will be worth it."**

Close by asking kids to think this week about the "Dueling Believers" characters who appeared in this session. Do these characters' positions make more—or less—sense than Christianity does? Encourage kids to keep asking questions, knowing that God is the God of faith and reason.

Are most of your young people wrestling with the fine points of apologetics? Are they running aground on the shoals of nihilistic existentialism? Probably not. The most common, garden-variety doubt among Christian kids in our culture may be a simple one: The nagging suspicion that Christianity may be true, but that it just isn't worth the sacrifice.

Look at it from your students' point of view. Compared with the Corvettes, condos, and cash this world has to offer, don't prayer and piety seem pretty pale? Money may not buy happiness, but a lot of our more pragmatic kids are willing to give it a try. If a few commandments get trampled in the process, so be it.

Abstinence, discipleship, self-control, purity, standing against the crowd—values like these sound awfully boring to most kids. Young people aren't used to thinking about the long term, and they don't have to when society offers instant gratification of most urges.

What can we do? Downplay the cost of following Jesus? Exaggerate the emptiness of non-Christian peers? This session does neither. It's designed to help you acknowledge kids' pragmatic doubts and paint a realistic picture of life with and without Christ. The rest is up to your students, as they begin to take a long-term look at a short-term world.

I'm Not Sure
It's Worth It

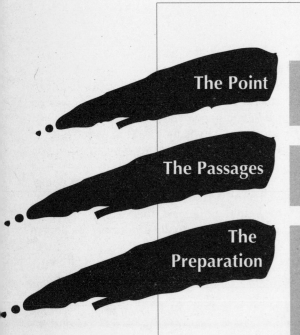

The Point	To help kids weigh the pleasures and consequences of sin against the rewards and costs of Christian discipleship.
The Passages	Matthew 7:13, 14; Hebrews 11:24-27; Galatians 5:19-23; Luke 9:23-25; Proverbs 10:28, 29; Ecclesiastes 12:1
The Preparation	You'll need the following: • Copies of "Lifestyles of the Rich and Faithless" (Student Sheet 23) • Newsprint and markers • Copies of "Truth about Consequences" (Student Sheet 24) • Pencils • Bibles • Masking tape

Lifestyles of the Rich and Faithless
Recognizing that Faith Doesn't Always Seem Worth It

Before you meet, give copies of "Lifestyles of the Rich and Faithless" (Student Sheet 23) to three budding actors from your group. If possible, rehearse the skit ahead of time. Then perform it to introduce today's topic. Encourage your performers to ham it up and to speak clearly.

After the skit, start the discussion with questions like these:

How would you summarize the philosophy of Buffy and Jody? (One possibility: Enjoy yourself no matter who you hurt, because this life is all there is.)

Do you think Buffy and Jody deserve to be successful? (Not if wealth is a reward for obeying God.)

Do you know of any famous or wealthy people who don't appear to be Christians? Any kids at school who seem to be having a good time even though they don't obey God? (There are plenty. Kids should be able to suggest several.)

Why does God let people who reject Him become successful and enjoy themselves? (Tough question. Let kids try, but don't offer a "right" answer.)

Let's say you're trying to live the way God wants you to. And it's not easy. Then you look around and see lots of people who couldn't care less about God. They're sinning and they're having a great time. They don't have to give anything up, or go to church, or read the Bible. What questions might you start asking yourself? (Why try to obey God? Why doesn't God punish them? Wouldn't it be okay if I live like they do now and then get serious when I'm old?)

Encourage kids to voice as many questions as they can. Then observe that most of these questions can be wrapped up in one: Is obeying God worth it? Explain that you'll be looking into that question today.

Is the Price Right?
Comparing Results of Living for God and Living for Yourself

Ask: **To decide whether something's worth it, what do we have to know?** (Answers will vary, but they'll probably boil down to two: How much it costs and what we get out of it.) **So let's look at two ways of living. We'll see how much they cost and what we get out of them.**

Read Matthew 7:13, 14. Discuss the fact that the narrow road is living God's way, following and obeying Christ; the wide road is living any way you please. The gates are like our choices to follow one way or the other.

Which road is more popular? (The wide one.)

Where do the roads lead? (God's way leads to life; our own way leads to destruction.)

If the wide road leads to destruction, why do so many people on it seem to be having a good time? (The destruction may not come until after they die.)

If the narrow road leads to life, how can some Christians die when they're young? (Christ is talking about eternal life in Heaven.)

Tell kids you're officially appointing them as "price checkers." **So what's the price of the narrow road?** (A harder life, fewer companions.) **What do you get out of it?** (Eternal life.) Ask the same questions about the wide road. Its benefit is an easier earthly life, but its cost is steep: destruction.

Keep track of "prices and payoffs" on a sheet of newsprint as you and your price checkers examine the following verses: Hebrews 11:24-27; Galatians 5:19-23; Luke 9:23-25; Proverbs 10:28, 29; John 10:10. When you're done you'll probably end up with a chart that looks something like this:

Price of God's Way: Low status, mistreatment, disgrace, giving up pleasures of sin and treasure and home (Hebrews 11:24-27); self-denial and following Christ daily, possible loss of life (Luke 9:23-25).

Payoffs of God's Way: Being part of God's people, honor of serving Christ, future reward (Hebrews 11:24-27); being able to develop love, joy, peace, patience, etc. (Galatians 5:19-23); salvation (Luke 9:23-25); hopes ultimately realized in Heaven, and having the Lord as our protector and strength on earth (Proverbs 10:28, 29); a full (abundant) life (John 10:10).

Price of Going Our Own Way: A tendency to sexual immorality, impurity, jealousy, rage, selfish ambition, etc., and not inheriting God's kingdom (Galatians 5:19-23); losing one's soul, or eternal death (Luke 9:23-25); not having our hopes ultimately fulfilled, and destruction (Proverbs 10:28, 29).

Payoffs of Going Our Own Way: Pleasures of sin for a short time (Hebrews 11:24-27); possibly gaining everything this world has to offer (Luke 9:23-25).

When your chart is complete, ask: **Which way of living do you think is the better value? Why?**
Kids may say God's way is worth more because the eternal price of sin is so high. But don't settle for an easy answer. Ask: **If the narrow way is obviously a better deal, why does the wide road look so tempting sometimes?**
Encourage kids to share their feelings about this. If possible, tell of a time when you thought the wide road looked pretty attractive. Note that even when we believe what the Bible says, eternal rewards and punishment can seem awfully far away—too far away to affect us. We need help to see that time flies, whether or not we're having fun.

Truth about Consequences
Remembering God in the Days of Our Youth

Pass out "Truth about Consequences" (Student Sheet 24). Have kids work on these individually. Allow plenty of time for students to think about these two hypothetical life choices and the results, and to express their opinions with drawings or symbols.
After a few minutes, gather the group and have volunteers show and explain their responses. On what did kids base their answers? Do any of the drawings or symbols reflect verses you just studied? Rather than trying to correct "wrong" answers, ask kids whether their responses agree or disagree with the prices and payoffs you identified earlier.
Most of us would probably agree that eternal life in Heaven is worth more than eternal death. But we tend to forget there's a connection between now and the future. That's why it can help to remind ourselves of the long-range view, the kind of view God takes.
Have a volunteer read Ecclesiastes 12:1, about remembering our Creator in the days of our youth. **We tend to forget God and how worthwhile His way really is. If you wanted to remind yourself this week that following Christ is**

worth it, how could you do it? (Let kids come up with ideas. Some possibilities: Remember something you drew on the "Truth about Consequences" sheet; think about how God has helped you or your family in the past; compare the shallow promises of a TV commercial with some promises in the Bible.)

Fun from A to Z
Showing That Non-Christians Don't Have All the Fun

Wrap up the session in a fun way, reminding kids that the Christian life isn't just standing around waiting to go to Heaven while the pagans party. As a matter of fact, Christians can have a good time, too, as part of a God-honoring life (see Proverbs 17:22).

Tape several sheets of newsprint to the walls or place paper on the floor. Split the group into two teams and give a marker to the captain of each team. The object: To list fun things Christians are free to do, each activity beginning with a different letter of the alphabet. The first team to write a word for every letter of the alphabet, or the team listing the most words in three minutes, wins. Here are a few examples:

A: Acting, avocado-eating, alpine skiing.
B: Baseball, boating, bird watching.
C. Computer games, calligraphy, catching fish.

When the lists are done, ask kids to put check marks by some of their favorite activities. Then offer the lists as a reference to the person in charge of planning social events for your group.

In an experiment conducted a few years ago by psychiatric researchers, several teenagers wore electronic pagers as they went about their daily routines. At odd moments the "beepers" would go off, signaling the kids to record in notebooks how they were feeling at the moment. The resulting diaries showed the young people's emotions were strong and changing several times a day, confirming the truism that adolescents are especially susceptible to emotional upheaval.

Christian kids are no different. They can find "spiritual" highs at church camps and retreats, only to lose them a few days later. They "go forward" to be saved, confess, rededicate themselves, declare their commitment to serving God—and after a few months of being "on fire," they can cool off.

What happens when they stop "feeling God's presence" and "having the joy of the Lord"? If they equate feelings with faith, they doubt. They doubt that their earlier emotions were real, or that God is even there. They may respond by tossing the faith that has disappointed them—or by stifling their "unspiritual" feelings.

This session can help bring kids' up-and-down emotions into the open, where you and the Bible can acknowledge them as part of life. For students who have faith and feelings mixed up, it could be very reassuring.

I've Lost the
Feeling

The Point

To help young people understand that it's normal for our feelings about God and the Christian life to change, and that those changes don't have to mean disaster for our faith.

The Passages

Selected Psalms; John 6:60-69

The Preparation

You'll need the following:
- Hymnals (one per student)
- Small prize (optional)
- Copies of "Mysteries!" (Student Sheets 25 and 26)
- Pencils
- Bibles

Singing Sword Drill
Admitting Our Feelings about God Aren't Always Positive

Pass out hymnals, one to each student. Explain that you're going to have a "sword drill"—but instead of seeing who can find Bible verses most quickly, kids will look up songs. Practice once by calling out the number of a hymn; whoever finds it first reads the title.

For the actual drill, though, you won't be calling out numbers. You'll ask kids to find hymn lyrics that reflect certain feelings about God. So they'll have to look a little harder. Start the contest and work your way through the following list.

1. Find some lyrics that remind you of how you felt about God when you first became a Christian.
2. Find words describing feelings that seem strange to you.
3. Find lyrics that reflect a way you've felt about Jesus.
4. Find words that describe how you feel right now.
5. Find an expression of a feeling you would like to feel but don't.
6. Find an emotion you felt last week.
7. Find a description of something you don't always feel about other Christians.

After each song or lyric is found, have its finder explain why it fits the description. For example, one student might pick words from "Joy to the World" or "Love Lifted Me" to reflect the excitement or gratitude he or she felt after receiving Christ. Another might choose "and now I am happy all the day" as a strange-sounding phrase.

If you like, award a small prize to the person who gave the most answers. Then ask: **Why don't all the songs in this book reflect the way we feel about God right now?** (The authors were describing how they felt when they wrote the songs, and we don't necessarily feel the same way at this moment.)

Let's say you feel really good about God today, and you write a song about those feelings. But a month from now you look at the song again and you don't want to sing it. You don't feel the same way about God. Is that possible? Why? (Our feelings about God, like all our feelings, change all the time.)

Our feelings about God do change. One day we can feel close to Him, and the next day He seems a million miles away. We're going to do a little detective work to figure out how that could happen.

Playing Detective
Discovering Why Our Feelings about God Can Change

Distribute copies of "Mysteries!" (Student Sheets 25 and 26). Have kids go over these cases in groups or individually and answer the questions. Then re-gather and discuss the results. Use the following information to supplement students' responses as needed.

The Case of the Rocky Mountain High
Tracey's experience isn't unusual. What happened to her at camp involved very strong feelings, and if we felt that strongly all the time we'd probably burn out. Her prayer indicates that she expected God to completely and instantly change her, which He hadn't promised to do. That led to disappointment. So did her plans to read the Bible for an hour every morning. Her expec-

tations were too high, especially when she hadn't been in the habit of reading the Bible at all. If she'd started more gradually and had been prepared for setbacks along the way, she might not have felt like such a failure.

Tracey's lack of supportive Christian friends made it hard to change her ways at school. She misses the two friends she met at camp, too, which adds to her depression. It all adds up to a deep valley after a mountaintop high.

The Case of the Sounds of Silence

Mario feels abandoned—by God and by the youth group. When his mother got cancer, Mario prayed that she would be healed. When she seemed to improve, he was overjoyed. Everything would be fine, Mario thought; God was proving His care for Mario's family by answering his prayer. Then his mother worsened and died. Mario's happiness was replaced by shock, then anger. Where was God?

The other kids in the youth group didn't help things. Their relationship with Mario was only on the surface. They didn't go out of their way to find out about the trouble he was going through, even when he stopped attending. Already bitter over his mother's death, he decided Christians were hypocrites. He felt he couldn't trust them or God. If one or two kids in the group had built good relationships with Mario, he might have made it through this crisis with his faith intact. He may still make it, but it will take time.

The Case of the Stranger in the Night

What happened to Keith isn't as dramatic as the cases of Tracey and Mario. But it's probably more like the emotional changes most of us go through.

Keith's dusty Bible is part of the answer. It's harder to maintain our feelings of closeness to God when we don't do anything to stay close to Him. Getting to know God through the Bible is only part of that, but it's an important one. The good feelings Keith got from the praise tape were also important, but they're not enough to base a relationship on.

The rest of the clues may not sound very spiritual, but they have a lot to do with Keith's feelings. He got a bad grade when he'd probably been expecting to do well; he feels hurt and angry that his boss yelled at him, and may be worried that he'll lose his job. He's also getting a cold—and physical stress affects our feelings. Add the fact that it's the middle of the night, a time when most of us don't think straight anyway, and you've got plenty of reasons for Keith's feelings to have changed.

These three people felt close to God, then far away. Who moved—the people or God?

Kids may say the people, or their feelings, did the changing. But how do they know that? How do they know our negative feelings don't drive God away? In the next step you'll look together for answers in the Bible.

Ups and Downs
Examining David's Changing Feelings about God

Step 3

Assign kids to look up and read aloud the following verses. Explain that the verses show how David felt about God as he wrote the Psalms.

David is one of the great heroes of the Bible, a man who really loved God. So we might think he was always happy, that his feelings about God never changed. To find out, we'll read these verses. After each verse is read, stand up if you think David was feeling "up" when he wrote it. Sit down if

you think David was feeling "down."

Here are the verses and their corresponding ups and downs:

Psalm 5:11, 12—Up
6:1-7—Down
9:1, 2—Up
10:1-4—Down
11:4-7—Up
13:1, 2—Down
16:5-11—Up

By the time all the verses have been read, your group may be tired of getting up and down, so tell them to sit back down for a rest. Discuss the reasons for David's shifting emotions (being pursued by enemies, being tired, seeing God protect him, worrying about what would happen next time, feeling that God was far away, remembering God's blessings, etc.).

Here was a man who had a strong relationship with God—yet He expressed some feelings that a lot of people wouldn't admit to in church. What were some of these "forbidden" feelings? (That God had forgotten him or was too slow in helping him; wanting revenge on enemies; being depressed about life.)

When David felt God was far away, what did he do? (Talked to God about it.) **How did God respond?** (He kept coming to David's aid.)

With all these ups and downs, why do you think the two of them stayed together? (God must have understood David's feelings and loved Him anyway; God kept coming to David's rescue; it probably helped David to honestly express his feelings to God; David based his faith on God, not on feelings.)

We can keep our changing feelings from capsizing our relationship with God, too. It helps if we put our feelings into perspective.

Staying Power
Putting Our Feelings about God into Perspective

Step 4

Read, or have students read, John 6:60-69. Ask kids to summarize what is going on in this scene. As needed, explain that the feelings of many of Jesus' followers have changed. They don't like what He's teaching, and now they are deserting Him. Jesus asks the 12 disciples whether they want to leave, too. Peter says, "Lord, to whom shall we go? You have the words of eternal life. We believe and know that you are the Holy One of God."

Why did Peter and the others stick with Jesus? (There was no place else to go, because Jesus is the only Way; there's only one God.)

It was knowing who God is, not feeling a certain way about Him, that kept Peter and the others with Jesus. It's the same with us. Our feelings are important, and God cares about them, but it's knowing who He is that's more important. That's because our feelings change—and He doesn't.

If you have time, have kids compare their relationship with God to a human friendship or romantic relationship. What happens if changeable feelings are more important than commitment to the other person? The relationship falls apart when the going's rough. Discuss how the maintenance of a friendship is like maintaining our closeness to God.

Wrap up the session by encouraging kids to keep track of their feelings about God this week. If you like, review the results next time you meet.

"I thought I was a Christian, but now I don't know. I can't remember the day I became one."

"I asked Jesus to save me, but nothing happened. I don't feel any different."

"I'm afraid I won't go to Heaven when I die. I keep doing things I know are wrong, so how could I possibly be a Christian?"

Once you believe in the need for salvation, doubting your own is a very unsettling experience. So much is at stake, and the Accuser is so busy. That's especially true for young people, many of whom are racked by guilt over "unconquered" sin or buffeted by sudden mood shifts. For others the problem is one of maturing, as they realize how shallow their childhood understanding of conversion has been.

This session is designed to give kids a fresh look at what the Bible says about the differences between those who are saved and those who aren't. Above all, you'll be encouraging your students to see God alone as the definer of who's "in" and who's "out," and to get things right with Him.

I'm Not Sure I'm Saved

The Point	To help students evaluate their spiritual standing according to Scripture, and to encourage them to change that standing if needed.
The Passages	James 2:14-20; John 3:16-18; Acts 16:29-31; I John 1:9-2:2; 2:9, 10; 3:16-20; Romans 8:31-39; 10:9-11
The Preparation	You'll need the following: • Coins in a sealed envelope • Chalkboard and chalk or newsprint and marker • Copies of "Map of the Kingdom" (Student Sheet 27) • Paper and pencils • Bibles

Positive I.D.
Seeing the Difficulty of Proving Who You Are

If possible, have kids sit in a circle or other pattern that allows them to see each other. Announce that you've been put in charge of a very rich man's estate, and you're here to give the inheritance to someone in the room. Hold up an envelope in which you've sealed some coins to show that you mean business.

Explain that the money will go to the person who is most convincing at proving his or her identity. You'll go around the circle, giving each student 30 seconds to prove who he or she is (if your group is too large, pick just a few students to do this). Evidence could include student I.D. cards, driver's licenses, signatures, testimony by others, ability to recite facts about one's life, sincerity of presentation, etc.

There's a catch, though: Since everybody wants the inheritance, kids should do their best to accuse each other of being fakes. After all, I.D. cards could be forged, witnesses could be lying, facts could be memorized.

When claims and counterclaims are finished and the dust has cleared, have kids vote to decide who was most convincing. Award the "inheritance" to that person. Then make the following application.

It can be pretty hard to prove who you are, especially when someone's accusing you of being a fake. It's the same way with our faith. Sometimes we start doubting whether we're really Christians. We may have said a certain prayer once when we were little, but now we're not sure we're saved after all. Why might a person start doubting like that?

Brainstorm possibilities, listing them on chalkboard or newsprint. Here are some: We keep sinning, and think a real Christian wouldn't do that; Satan accuses us to mix us up; we can't remember when we became Christians; someone else doubts our sincerity; we're not sure what a Christian is.

Ask kids whether they've experienced any of these. How did it feel? Observe that the question of one's salvation is the most important one we can wrestle with—or get settled.

Driver's Test
Trying to Test Ourselves for Christian Commitment

Ask how many kids have taken the test to get their driver's licenses. Explain, or let them explain, that the test comes in two parts: the written one and the road test. The written one measures knowledge; the road test shows our ability to put the knowledge into practice.

Let's say you're inventing a test that will show whether or not you're a Christian. Will it be more like the written test or the road test? Will you test knowledge or practice?

Kids may choose one or both. Read James 2:14-20 to show that a Christian is to believe *and* practice. In a way, the road test shows whether we really mean what we put down on the written test.

But we run into a problem here. If your test measures whether you're doing everything the Bible says to do, how can you pass? (You can't. You'd have to be perfect.)

Some of us try to measure ourselves that way. We fall short, either on knowing all the right things (like exactly when we became Christians) or on doing them. No wonder we can worry that we aren't Christians after all. There's got to be another way.

You Are Here
Finding a Better Way to See Where We Are

Step 3

Distribute copies of "Map of the Kingdom" (Student Sheet 27). Go over the instructions with kids and have them complete the sheet. When they're done, they should have key words from the following passages in these spots on the map:

John 3:16-18; Acts 16:29-31; Romans 10:9-11—Entrance
I John 2:9, 10; 3:16-20—General Way of Life
I John 1:9-2:2—Cleansing River
Romans 8:31-39—Protective Wall

Discuss the results. Have volunteers share where they marked their locations on the map and why.

Our "Entrance" verses make it clear how we get into this Kingdom. If you're trusting Christ for your salvation, you've entered—whether or not you can recall the day you entered, whether or not you felt a certain way when you did it. Once we're inside, God expects us to recognize His authority by following His Word. When we fail and confess, He offers forgiveness so that we can continue to grow as citizens of His Kingdom.

In Your Own Words
Making Sure We Know How to Become Christians

Step 4

If you have time, ask kids to write in 25 words or less how a person becomes a Christian. But to make sure they aren't just parroting phrases they don't understand, tell them they must do it in their own words. Don't allow direct quoting of Bible verses, or use of terms such as born again, faith, sin, saved, receive, accept, or "take Jesus into your heart." Write your own version ahead of time to see what a challenge it can be, and to help you evaluate kids' paraphrases when volunteers read theirs to the group.

Settling Up
Choosing to Believe or Reject God's Promises

Step 5

End your session with a time of silent prayer. Kids who have been reassured of their salvation can use this time to thank God. If you wish, as heads are bowed, read the following statement by author John White (*The Fight,* InterVarsity Press, 1976):

"When you became a Christian, a number of extremely important events took place both in Heaven and in your own body. You may not have felt anything. Christians have widely differing experiences, ranging from intense emotions to nothing at all. You may not even be able to say when you became a Christian. All you may know is that at this moment you acknowledge the Jesus of history to be your Savior and your God."

Invite students who don't have this assurance to talk with you afterward. Then close with a prayer of your own.

Sign on The Doubted Line

Initials

_____ 1. This person has wondered why God doesn't always seem to answer prayer.

_____ 2. This person and I said the words "I'm sure!" together five times fast.

_____ 3. This person may have some doubts, but would rather not say.

_____ 4. This person has wondered at least once whether it's worth it to live the way the Bible tells you to.

_____ 5. This person knows someone who doubts that God exists.

_____ 6. This person doesn't feel exactly the same way about God every day.

_____ 7. This person doubts that the leader of this group is always right.

_____ 8. This person doesn't always feel like saying what the apostle Paul does in II Timothy 1:12. (Look up the verse to find out.)

_____ 9. This person has a relative who isn't 100% sure about Christianity.

_____ 10. This person has wondered how God feels about people who doubt Him.

Shocking Secrets
by Verne Becker

For a minute, I could hardly believe my ears.

I was sitting there in my study-and-prayer group with my closest friends, none of whom were new to the Christian faith. I looked up to these people. I had great respect for their spiritual wisdom and maturity. But here they were, one by one, openly sharing deep doubts and fears about God.

One of them said, "I have trouble believing God's really there. It seems that one bad thing after another keeps happening to me, and if God really cares, why doesn't He do something about it? Why don't things ever seem to get better for me?"

"I really struggle in my prayer life," said another. "All I feel sometimes is God's silence."

Still another friend said, "I wonder if God is really at work in the world. Sometimes I see glimpses of Him in other people, but people are human and they let me down. I don't see God getting through any other way."

At first I just wanted to say, "Wait a minute, guys! Hey, we all know God is real—we've been taught that for years. The Bible says so, and that's where we can hear God's voice if we take time to read it." But before the words came out I stopped myself. I knew they'd heard that argument thousands of times before.

Instead, I just listened. I felt the pain of their questioning, their yearning for truth, their desire to *feel* God and not just believe in a vacuum. And I also realized that I feel all those same things sometimes. There have been situations when I've felt that God let me down, or when I've ached for His presence and felt nothing.

As I left the meeting, I almost felt overwhelmed with doubt myself. *If these people, whose faith I respect so deeply, are expressing such doubts, what hope is there for me? Are we all just faking Christianity when we doubt? Are we all hypocrites?*

By the time I got home I had made my decision: *No, I'm not a hypocrite.* When I stopped to think about it, I realized that the Christians who turn me off most are not the doubters, but exactly the opposite. The real hypocrites are often those who *never* express any doubts or questions toward God—the ones who seem to deny reality by saying that life is always wonderful and that everything always works out great.

I've experienced enough pain myself to know that things don't always work out great. I guess I'm not a La-De-Da Christian. I'm more drawn to people like those in my prayer group—people who truly believe, but who aren't afraid to express their honest feelings toward God.

Excerpted from "Not Afraid to Doubt," U *magazine,* © 1988.

Get This Straight

Straighten out each of the following twisted statements by checking the verses in Hebrews 11 and making corrections in the spaces provided.

1. Faith is believing in something that probably isn't true.

(11:1, 2) _____

2. If you're a good Christian, you don't need any faith to believe that God made the universe.

(11:3) _____

3. If you want to start a relationship with God, just wait until He proves to you that He's there.

(11:6) _____

4. All the people who truly believed God's promises in the Old Testament saw those promises fulfilled before they died.

(11:13) _____

5. If God promises you something, it only comes true *after* you die.

(11:29, 30) _____

6. Only really good, respectable people can have faith.

(11:31) _____

7. Faith has no practical value.

(11:32-34) _____

8. If you have faith, God will make sure nobody hurts you.

(11:35-38) _____

9. If you don't see God answering your prayers, either He doesn't like you or you don't have enough faith.

(11:39) _____

Dueling Believers

1. Starla Wonder (a giggly airhead)

"Oh, I think there's something out there, don't you? I mean, like, the planets control what we do. If you read your horoscope, you'll see what I mean. Like mine today said, 'You will get out of bed this morning.' How did they know that? And then it said, 'Avoid large steel objects hurtling toward your head at speeds of more than 600 miles per hour.' Wow! Sure enough, I avoided anything like that and I survived! It's obviously, like, *true*, you know?"

2. Kerry Reasoner (calm, careful)

"Astrology is illogical. Logic and reason are the only things that make sense. If I can't reason it out, it's not true. Therefore, my brain is the center of the universe. Everything I do must be based on reason alone. I think I'm hungry, but all options must be considered. But if all options are considered, I will never have time to eat. And if I do eat, is it more logical to have a cheeseburger or some pizza? Why not spinach? This could take a while."

3. Kurt McKult (weird, spaced out)

"We must forget reason. The great New Age guru Shreelee Rajwheelie tells us that only ideas which make no sense make any sense at all. We must follow our guru and get in touch with our past lives, wear crystals in our underwear, and be kind to aliens from outer space. And buy several copies of the guru's new book, *Give Me All Your Money*, available for $14.95 at fine bookstores everywhere."

4. Charlotte Darwin (very sure of herself)

"Save your money. Religion is no longer necessary. Science explains the world without any need for God. We have proven beyond a shadow of a doubt that man came from sea slugs, sea slugs came from slime, slime came from chemicals, and chemicals came from the earth. The earth came from chemicals, which came from slime, which came from sea slugs, which—no, wait a minute. But trust me. I was there when it happened."

5. Parr D. Animal (loud and rowdy)

"Man, I don't know where the world came from, and I don't care. Just give me a six-pack and some wheels with a good compact disc player and I'm happy. That's what counts, feeling good. You only go around once in life, so you've got to grab for all the potato chips you can. And money. Rock and roll forever! Let's party!"

6. Liv N. Letliv (always smiling)

"It doesn't really matter what you believe, now does it? Just be sincere. All roads lead to Heaven. We can't really know what's true, can we? I wouldn't try to tell anyone what to believe. Unless you believe that there's only one true faith. Then I'd have to knock you silly with a baseball bat. That might teach you to be more tolerant."

Lifestyles of The Rich and Faithless

ANNOUNCER (loud, excited voice): Hello! I'm Robbing Leech! Welcome to *Lifestyles of the Rich and Faithless,* where each week we bring you a glimpse of the most glamorous, most fabulously wealthy, most incredibly successful, most selfishly obnoxious people in the world! This week we're here at the fantastically sensational estate of the amazingly young teenage trillionaires, Buffy and Jody McMastercard! Hello, Buffy and Jody!

BUFFY (snooty): Oh, hello, you television person.

JODY (also snooty): Let's get on with this, shall we? I have to go shopping this afternoon.

ANNOUNCER: And what are you going to buy?

JODY: Something bright and tropical that fits me perfectly.

ANNOUNCER: A new shirt?

JODY: No. Hawaii.

ANNOUNCER: How fantastically sensational! Tell me, Buffy, how did you and Jody get all those trillions of dollars?

BUFFY: We started by smuggling illegal drugs across the border. Then we took that money and bought a company that makes toxic waste and dumps it in people's back yards when they're asleep.

ANNOUNCER: But that's terrible! Doesn't your conscience bother you, knowing you've ruined so many people's lives?

JODY: Are you kidding? We didn't need our consciences. So we sold those, too.

ANNOUNCER: But surely you've found that, even with all your money, deep down you're not happy. You feel empty inside.

BUFFY: Where did you come from, Bozo? We're having a great time. No worries, no hassles. We're going to do whatever we please for the rest of our lives. And we'll drive our Porsches over anybody who gets in the way.

ANNOUNCER: But after you die, then what? Don't you think you should prepare for the next life?

JODY: Why bother? As far as we're concerned, this is all the life we'll ever need. We fly our private jet to all the best rock concerts, we know every celebrity in Hollywood, and we have live-in dermatologists so we never get a single zit.

ANNOUNCER: But aren't you worried about what will happen someday when you meet God?

BUFFY: Who?

ANNOUNCER: You know—God. The Creator of the universe.

JODY: Never heard of him.

BUFFY: And we don't want to. We know so many people already, we had to buy the Superdome just so we could have parties. We don't want to know this God fellow.

JODY: Right. Who needs him? We don't need anybody but ourselves.

BUFFY: And our accountant.

JODY: So get lost, will you? We're going to buy your TV show just so we can cancel it. You're getting on our nerves.

ANNOUNCER (still loud): I don't know why! Tune in next week for another excitingly depressing look at people who spend more on a haircut than you'll make in your entire life! This is Robbing Leech for *Lifestyles of the Rich and Faithless!*

Truth about Consequences

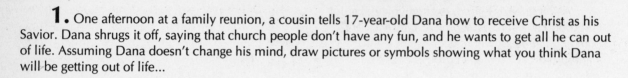

1. One afternoon at a family reunion, a cousin tells 17-year-old Dana how to receive Christ as his Savior. Dana shrugs it off, saying that church people don't have any fun, and he wants to get all he can out of life. Assuming Dana doesn't change his mind, draw pictures or symbols showing what you think Dana will be getting out of life...

a. A year from now

b. Ten years from now

c. Fifty years from now

d. Two hundred years from now

2. Kellie, 16, has been a Christian since she was in the third grade. She's not perfect (she has a habit of being sarcastic), but she's really grateful to Christ for what He did for her on the cross. She wants to serve Him by helping other people, maybe as a medical missionary. If she does that, she'll have to move away from her family, give up most of her possessions, and work with people who are sick and dying. Assuming she does that, draw pictures or symbols showing what you think Kellie will be getting out of life . . .

a. A year from now

b. Ten years from now

c. Fifty years from now

d. Two hundred years from now

Mysteries!

In each of the following cases, some feelings about God were lost. See whether you can figure out what happened to them.

The Case of the Rocky Mountain High

Tracey went to a Christian camp in Colorado last summer. The river rafting and horseback riding were fun, and she met two new friends she really liked. But the high point for her was a spiritual one.

Tracey had known for a long time that she hadn't been leading the kind of life a Christian should. Some things the camp speaker said on the last night of camp really got to her, and when she returned to her cabin she started to cry. Her counselor asked what was wrong, and Tracey let the whole story spill out. That night Tracey rededicated her life to Christ. She felt so good about it, so clean, that she wanted to tell the whole world. Things were going to be different now.

But three weeks later, Tracey was back in the same old rut. Those wonderful feelings about God seemed to have evaporated, and she felt worse than ever. What had happened?

> The Clues:
> 1. The new friends Tracey made at camp live in Montana, and she's from Texas.
> 2. When Tracey rededicated her life, she prayed, "Lord, just take over my life. I'll do anything you want. Make me be the right kind of person."
> 3. On the way back from camp, Tracey decided that from now on she would get up an hour earlier each day and read the Bible through in six months.
> 4. Most of Tracey's old friends from school aren't Christians.

Your Conclusions?

The Case of the Sounds of Silence

Mario used to be part of the youth group at church. The other kids were impressed by him; he seemed so serious about being a Christian. Mario's parents didn't go to church, so the rest of the group didn't know much about them. At first the other kids didn't notice when Mario started missing meetings. When it became obvious, no one seemed to know where he was. The youth director said something about Mario having problems at home, but after a while the group quit asking about him.

The other day one of the kids in the group saw Mario at school and invited him to a church concert. "Church?" Mario said angrily. "Man, don't talk to me about church. You can keep your church, and your God, too." What had happened?

> The Clues:
> 1. Mario really had been serious about being a Christian.
> 2. Mario's mother had cancer. He prayed for her, and for a while it looked like she was going to recover. But one night she went to the hospital, and a week later she died.
> 3. When Mario was invited to the church concert, it was the first time in four months that he'd heard from anyone in the youth group.

Your Conclusions?

Mysteries!

(continued)

The Case of the Stranger in the Night

Just last week Keith was thinking about how great it was to be a Christian. He was in his room, listening to a tape of praise songs his brother had gotten him for his birthday, and was surprised to find himself getting into the music. He didn't usually do that. The next day he felt really peaceful, even when he was taking a pop quiz in geometry. *This is fantastic,* he thought. *I feel so close to God I could almost reach out and touch Him.*

But last night Keith woke up suddenly, looking around in the moonlight. He lay there for a while, and slowly a cloud of anxiety seemed to form in the room. God was a stranger now. If He was there at all, He must have been on the other side of the galaxy. The tape of praise songs was just a piece of plastic. Keith felt more alone than he had in a long, long time. What had happened?

The Clues:
1. Keith's Bible, on the shelf near his bed, has a lot of dust on it.
2. Keith got a low grade on his geometry quiz.
3. Yesterday, at the dry cleaners' where he works after school, Keith was yelled at by the boss for mixing up two orders.
4. Keith is coming down with a cold.

Your Conclusions?

Map of The Kingdom

Where is the Kingdom of God? It's where God is given His rightful place as King. Try using this symbolic map to help answer the question of whether or not you've entered the Kingdom through faith in Jesus Christ.

First, look up the Bible passages listed. Decide whether each passage has something to say about the entrance to the Kingdom, the protective wall around it, the river that keeps citizens clean, or the general way of life throughout the Kingdom. Write a key word or two from each passage on the part of the map it describes.

Then think about where you stand on the map today. Are you far beyond the wall? Just outside the entrance? Just inside the entrance? Further inside? Needing a bath in the river? Wherever it is, mark the spot with an X.

Passages to look up: John 3:16-18   I John 2:9, 10; 3:16-20

Acts 16:29-31   I John 1:9-2:2

Romans 10: 9-11   Romans 8:31-39